Ottawa

A Contemporary Portrait

**Sponsored by the
Ottawa-Carleton Board of Trade**

Ottawa

A Contemporary Portrait

By Sue Baker

Featuring the photography of Ari Tapiero

Profiles by Yvonne Jeffery Hope and Vivian Astroff

Ottawa
A Contemporary Portrait

Sponsored by the
Ottawa-Carleton Board of Trade
350 Albert Street
Suite 1710
Ottawa, Ontario K1R 1A4
(613) 236-3631
Fax: (613) 236-7498
E-mail: info@board-of-trade.org
Web site: www.board-of-trade.org

By *Sue Baker*
Corporate profiles by *Yvonne Jeffery Hope*
and Vivian Astroff
Featuring the photography of *Ari Tapiero*

Community Communications, Inc.
Publishers: *Ronald P. Beers and James E. Turner*

Staff for *Ottawa: A Contemporary Portrait*
Publisher's Sales Associate: *C. Brian Rhodes*

Executive Editor *James E. Turner*
Managing Editor *Linda Moeller Pegram*
Design Director *Camille Leonard*
Designer *Chris Elliott*
Photo Editors *Chris Elliott and*
Linda M. Pegram
Production Manager *Cindy Lovett*
Editorial Assistants *Katrina Williams and*
Kari Collin
Sales Assistant *Annette R. Lozier*
Proofreader *Wynona B. Hall*
Accounting Services *Sara Ann Turner*
Printing Production *Frank Rosenberg/GSAmerica*

Community Communications, Inc.
Montgomery, Alabama

James E. Turner, Chairman of the Board
Ronald P. Beers, President
Daniel S. Chambliss, Vice President

©1997 Community Communications
All Rights Reserved
Published 1997
Printed in Canada
First Edition
Library of Congress Catalog Number: 97-36178
ISBN: 1-885352-74-3

Table of Contents

Our Capital Home

Ottawa, Canada's capital, is a city of rich history, natural beauty, diverse culture and leading-edge technology and innovation. Cosmopolitan and modern, we have big-league sports, world-class stages, a host of museums and attractions, superb education and health care and a strong high-tech and entrepreneurial sector. Yet, Ottawa is tranquil and natural, with waterways, parks and quiet paths for cycling and walking, and is home to many of Canada's national monuments and heritage sites. While over a million people live and work here, we feel a strong sense of community. Steeped in history, Ottawa is proud of our past and we're building a bright future.

Capital History–
Legends, Glamour, Politics & Intrigue

Ottawa's rich and storied past includes legends of the French explorer Samuel de Champlain, the lumber barons of "Bytown," the building of the Rideau Canal (a 19th-century engineering marvel still in use today), extraordinary war efforts and even a Titanic connection! Politicians, royalty and brilliant minds have left marks here; our historical sites resonate with the echoes of capital history and tradition.

Capital Living–
A Place for All Seasons

In Ottawa, every season's a celebration! The colours of our landscape change as the pages of the calendar turn. In Ottawa, your senses come alive, all year round! Ottawa is also a capital place in all the seasons of life. Our education system is superb, from our public and private schools to our colleges and universities, and our medical facilities are world-class. Homes to suit a wide variety of needs and budgets are found in close-knit neighbourhoods, and "child-friendly" Ottawa puts kids first!

Capital Sights–
You Won't Believe Your Eyes!

See the nation's collection of art–explore the history of aviation–marvel at the wonders of science and technology–walk among the dinosaurs–all in the museums of Ottawa! There's so much to see–our waterways are perfect for a boat cruise in summer or for skating on sparkling winter nights. Double-decker buses, bicycle rickshaws, a steam train and hot air balloons offer unique tours. The historic Byward Market and other charming districts are ideal for shopping or enjoying the patio scene. And, of course, visits to Ottawa should always include a tour behind the scenes of Canada's political seat of power, Parliament Hill.

Capital Arts & Entertainment–
Our World's a Stage!

From the excitement of NHL hockey to music superstars, live theatre, dance and the symphony, the world's greatest performers entertain on Ottawa's world-class stages. Our arts community is strong and vibrant, and capital nightlife is legendary. (Ottawa is the home town of music superstar Alanis Morissette!) And we sure know how to throw a party–our seasonal festivals draw millions to the capital each year!

Capital Culture–
A Global Community

Ottawa truly is a "global village," and we're proud of our diverse mix of culture. We celebrate our roots with a rainbow of cultural festivals, and Canada Day (our national holiday) at Parliament Hill is a major celebration of national pride. All denominations are respected here; service clubs and volunteerism are also an important part of our lives. And we're a "connected" community, with a highly computer-literate population reaching out to the world through the Internet.

Capital Hosts–
Be Our Guest!

"Bienvenue–Welcome to Ottawa!" Over 5 million people visit Canada's capital every year, and our hotels, restaurants and tourism organizations have perfected the fine art of making you feel right at home. The capital also has modern and functional spaces for conferences, conventions, trade shows and business entertaining. And, with our international airport, rail and road links, Ottawa is so accessible!

Capital Business Connections–
On Track with Trade

Ottawa has the business connections you need! In Canada's capital, federal government departments are easily accessible, and our technology transfer system is one of the most advanced in the world. We're in the business of doing business, and organizations like the Ottawa-Carleton Board of Trade, the Ottawa-Carleton Economic Development Corporation, the Ottawa-Carleton Research Institute and many others are helping companies establish roots and grow towards international success.

PART TWO 126

CHAPTER NINE, 102

Capital Innovators–
The Leading Edge in Technology

We're known as "Silicon Valley North" for good reason; Ottawa is one of Canada's most important centres for technological innovation. Companies like Nortel, MITEL Corporation, Newbridge Networks, Digital Equipment Corporation, Corel Corporation, Cognos Incorporated and hundreds of other high-tech firms based here are making a global impact on technology. Our life sciences and biotechnology sectors are flourishing, and our research facilities and resources are among the best in the world. In the nation's capital, the 21st century is in clear view!

CHAPTER TEN, 116

Capital Growth–
Thriving on Enterprise & Change

Ottawa is experiencing a remarkable period of growth and diversity with a healthy economy, a highly educated workforce and a wellspring of entrepreneurial spirit. Transportation links are being improved, resources like water and electricity are plentiful and we offer competitive rates for office and commercial space. Be a part of our "capital gains!"

128-129

Ottawa-Carleton Board of Trade

CHAPTER ELEVEN, 130

Networks

CHAPTER TWELVE, 144

High Technology & Manufacturing

CHAPTER THIRTEEN, 164

The Business Community

CHAPTER FOURTEEN, 182

Health Care, Education
& the Public Sector

CHAPTER FIFTEEN, 198

The Marketplace,
Hospitality & Attractions

CHAPTER SIXTEEN, 210

Real Estate & Construction

Foreword

We used to think of Ottawa as a government town, a region
where civil servants dominated the employment landscape. No more.
Today's Ottawa boasts a thriving entrepreneurial economy where over
80 per cent of the community works in the private sector. Where over
two-thirds of all Canadian telecommunications research and development is conducted. Where over 5 million visitors come to view our
tourism attractions or attend a convention. From the lumber town of
the 1800s to a world-class high-technology centre, Canada's capital
has plenty to offer. Make no mistake though; we are still the seat of
the government. As the capital, the community has garnered many
benefits, including a quality of life unmatched by any Canadian city.
The Ottawa-Carleton Board of Trade, the metro Ottawa Chamber
of Commerce, is pleased to present this testimonial to our region
during our 140th anniversary. When we began in 1857, we had
a vision for a beautiful, world-class city that was driven by the
private sector. As you read through the book, you will see that this
goal has been accomplished.

Willy Bagnell
President
Ottawa-Carleton
Board of Trade

Photo by Ari Tapiero

Preface

When I first moved to the Ottawa area nearly 10 years ago, I knew I had found my "place to call home." Raised in a small northern Ontario city, I'd also lived in some of Canada's larger metropolitan areas. I fell in love with Ottawa's unique mix of cosmopolitanism and natural beauty; its big-city offerings and small-town friendliness.

The capital's wide open spaces, protected greenspace and flowing rivers appeal to my nature-loving side, while its well-groomed cityscape, heritage buildings, sports and entertainment scene and arts community satisfy my need for metropolitan life. The wanderer in me loves the fact that I can drive to visit a different town or city in an afternoon, or board an international flight and explore the globe. As a parent, the fact that Ottawa is clean, safe, child-friendly and culturally rich has made it the right place for me to raise my family.

This book is, in large part, a testament to Ottawa's advances in high technology. The capital is in the midst of an unprecedented growth period, not only from an economic standpoint, but also in terms of the breakthroughs made here in technology that benefit people around the world. Without question, the biggest challenge in writing this book was to keep up to date with the exciting changes and positive developments that happen here on a daily basis. A substantial amount of research was performed by accessing information about our city, its companies and organizations via the Internet, and these resources are added proof of our technologically advanced society.

In the writing of this book, I've had enthusiastic help from so many members of the community and its organizations. In particular, I'd like to thank the staff of the Ottawa-Carleton Board of Trade, the Ottawa-Carleton Economic Development Corporation, the Ottawa Tourism and Convention Authority and the National Capital Commission for their prompt, cheerful and well-researched responses to my queries. Special thanks also to my editor, Linda Pegram at Community Communications, for her enthusiasm and professionalism. And the support and encouragement of my husband, John Luckock, my children, James and Katie Porobic, and my parents, June and Fred Baker, have given me the opportunity to reach yet another goal.

I hope that, in reading this book, you will be intrigued by the remarkable quality of life, the endless opportunities and the success stories that are part of our heritage. We invite you to come to Ottawa to share in, and be part of, capital history in the making.

Sue Baker

A Contemporary Portrait
PART ONE

OTTAWA INTERNATIONAL
**Antique & Classic
Boat Show**
HERE AT DOWS LAKE   AUGUST 8, 9 & 10

Photo by Ari Tapiero

CHAPTER ONE

Our Capital Home

What do people look for in "a place to call
home"? Certainly, as we stand on the brink of the
new millennium, we look for all that is modern—
in our homes, in our workplaces, in our
schools, in our recreation. We want the best
that our age of information and technology
can offer to make our lives easier, more
productive, more profitable, more successful.

Photo by Ari Tapiero

Previous page **One of the most popular spots for panoramic views of the Parliament Buildings and the Ottawa River is Nepean Point, where a statue of explorer Samuel de Champlain towers over the cityscape.**

W e want our children to have the best education possible, to grow up in a place that is safe and community oriented. We want to introduce them to a world of cultural diversity. We want a solid foundation from which we can strive for excellence, a place where opportunity for personal and financial growth is plentiful, somewhere we can raise our families, build our businesses, reach our potentials, fulfil our dreams.

Home, of course, means so much more. Home is a place where we can rest and revitalize our spirit, connect with our families, socialize with our friends and express ourselves through the arts or through recreation. We all seek a haven from our busy workday worlds. Inside most of us, there's a yearning for the simpler pleasures in life: a peaceful walk through the forest, a lazy summer day's fishing, a glorious sunset over the mountains, an ice-skating party with our children. These basic human needs are often hard to fulfil in an urban setting. We long for the old; we demand the new.

In Ottawa, the fourth largest urban centre in Canada, it's our way of life, for we truly have the best of both worlds. Situated in the province of Ontario, the capital of Canada is set along the convergence of three ancient waterways: the Ottawa, Rideau and Gatineau Rivers, across from the city of Hull in Quebec. Our region encompasses nearly 1,800 square miles, with a population of 1 million people. We're less than an hour's drive from the border at New York, a short drive or flight from Montreal or Toronto, and our international airport serves over 2.5 million travellers each year with ready connections to major cities in North America.

Our high standards and quality of living have been recognized around the world. Ottawa consistently places on the top-10 lists of "best cities" surveys; in 1995, we placed sixth in the world for quality of living in an international study by a Swiss-based research firm, the Corporate Resources Group, and for three consecutive years, the capital was ranked among the top-5 Canadian business centres in the "Best Cities, Report on Business" survey by Canada's national newspaper, the *Globe and Mail*.

There's a cosmopolitan feel to the capital, something reminiscent of the great cities of Europe. Our historic sites, particularly the signature silhouette of the neo-Gothic Parliament Buildings, stand proudly beside stunning examples of modern architecture such as the world-renowned National Gallery of Canada and the Canadian Museum of Civilization. Charming neighbourhoods abound—the historic downtown Byward Market with its fresh fruit and vegetable vendors, buskers and bicycle rickshaws, "Little Italy" on Preston Street, Chinatown in Somerset Heights. Our downtown area is revitalized and vibrant, with restoration and new development designed to come together in a harmonious blend. The picturesque Sparks Street Mall is devoted to pedestrians, with shops, outdoor patios and music in the air. The Bank Street Promenade, Elgin Street, the Glebe and Somerset Village have preserved the flavour of the "downtowns" of old. And Ottawa has 70 major shopping centres, along with hundreds of gift shops and retail stores.

As the seat of federal government, major political decisions and debates happen here every day; our prime minister and Parliament conduct the nation's business from Ottawa. Like our American counterpart, Washington, D.C., we are home to many foreign embassies and are the headquarters for the highest levels of government departments. Tourism is also a traditional stronghold. Over 5 million people visit the capital every year, and we are strengthening our position as one of the most popular convention destinations in North America.

We like to think of ourselves as "team players" in Ottawa. Sports and recreation play an important part in our lives, whether it's the "big leagues" or the "Little Leagues." The new 18,500-seat Corel Centre is home to the NHL Ottawa Senators Hockey Club and also hosts international sporting events, major concerts and family shows year-round. Along with our NHL team, we have a Triple-A baseball franchise, the Ottawa Lynx, as well as roller hockey, a top-notch junior hockey team, and more. There are numerous superb recreational facilities in the capital, dozens of golf courses and tennis courts, and literally hundreds of amateur sports organizations and clubs. There are seven ski hills within minutes of the city, and we have miles and miles of cross-country ski trails. We can leave the downtown core and in minutes, find ourselves fishing on the banks of the Ottawa River.

Photo by Ari Tapiero

Ottawa's culturally rich environment allows children to learn about the world, right here at home. Courtesy Canadian Tourism Commission. Photo by Mike Pinder.

Opposite page **Arts and entertainment thrive here; Ottawa's world-class stages play host to performances for every taste. Photo by Ari Tapiero.**

Our National Capital Commission has carefully protected the "greenspace" that is so important to the human spirit and has incorporated it into our daily lives. The Ottawa, Rideau and Gatineau Rivers, the Rideau Canal, Gatineau Park, the miles of cycling and nature trails within the city–all keep us grounded and close to nature. Over 42,000 acres of what we call the "Greenbelt" winds its way around the city, and ensures we'll never become a concrete jungle.

Arts and culture also shape who we are. The National Arts Centre presents concerts, the symphony, the ballet, touring Broadway musicals and contemporary artists from around the globe. The Ottawa Congress Centre, Centrepointe Theatre and the Civic Centre at Lansdowne Park are other popular entertainment venues. We have many local theatre troupes, and our National Capital Commission offers a summer concert series each

year. And, across the river, the new Casino de Hull is a dramatic and glamorous addition to our big-city offerings. Ottawa, as Canada's capital, is home to many of the nation's museums, including the Museum of Civilization, the Museum of Science and Technology, the Museum of Nature, the Royal Canadian Mint, the National Aviation Museum, the Canadian War Museum, the National Gallery of Canada and the National Archives of Canada–the repository for the country's historic records and artifacts.

Ottawa is a hotbed of talent, too; entertainers Rich Little, Paul Anka, Alex Trebek, Bryan Adams and Alanis Morissette, actors Matthew Perry and William Shatner, respected journalists Peter Jennings and Keith Morrison, and many other internationally known personalities have called Ottawa "home." Olympic medalists Glenroy Gilbert, Elizabeth Manley, Carolyn

Waldo and many others hail from the capital, and got the first "taste" of their sport right here in Ottawa.

And while over a million people live and work here, most of us call our neighbours by name. We are a community in every sense of the word, and our community is diverse. Our closeness to the province of Quebec means that many of us are able to speak two languages, English and French. We celebrate our origins with a rainbow of cultural festivals throughout the year, such as Italian Week, the Greek Festival, Féte-Caribe, the Odawa Powwow and many more. And our national holiday, Canada Day, is a celebration of Canada on Parliament Hill.

Ottawa is on the cutting edge of communications and information technology; in fact, we've been dubbed "Silicon Valley North," with internationally respected companies like Nortel, Digital, Newbridge Networks, Mitel Corporation, Corel Corporation and some 700 other high-tech firms making a global impact on technology. They're here because it's good business; they're here because our population is highly educated and technologically advanced. Ottawa's high-tech industry continues to experience growth, generating some $10 billion annually and growing at an estimated rate of 20 per cent per year. As an example, both Nortel and Newbridge have announced major expansion plans which will create a combined 9,000 new high-tech jobs in Ottawa by the year 2000. As many as 15,000 spin-off jobs may result, giving the local economy yet another boost.

We're also making breakthroughs in the fields of biotechnology, life sciences and medical research, with over $350 million invested each year in research and development in the life sciences field alone. We have the new Ottawa Life Sciences Council, pioneering work at the University of Ottawa Heart Institute and the Loeb Medical Research Centre, a broad range of specialized, general and teaching hospitals and over 85 private sector companies specializing in life sciences. The National Research Council of Canada is based in the capital; it's where the first pacemaker was developed and holds one of the most accurate clocks in the world! The nation's capital is also home to the head offices of many of the country's associations and organizations involved in life sciences and medicine.

Our institutes of higher education play a major role in the success of our high-tech and life sciences sectors. The University of Ottawa specializes in medicine, engineering and law; Carleton University offers a broad range of graduate and undergraduate programs, including engineering, architecture, business and journalism; Algonquin College provides theory and practical training in health care, business, computer sciences and more. Our publicly funded school boards set high standards in education, with low student/teacher ratios. There are over 275 public schools in Ottawa as well as numerous private schools offering specialized programs. As a result, Ottawa's population is highly educated and computer-literate; we also have one of the highest income levels per capita in the country.

We have an incredibly strong entrepreneurial sector, partly due to the strength of our major industries, but also attributable to the work of organizations like the Ottawa-Carleton Board of Trade, the Ottawa-Carleton Economic Development Corporation, the Ottawa-Carleton Research Institute, the Ottawa Life Sciences Council, and the Ottawa Tourism and Convention Authority. These proactive groups foster a healthy business environment through cooperation, communication, research and marketing.

People from all walks of life, from all over the world, have found Ottawa not only a fabulous place to visit, but have liked our view, our vision, so much that they've made it their "place to call home." We hope you will, too. ∎

Opposite page **The bustling downtown core is a sign of economic health. Tourism is one of Ottawa's biggest industries; some 5 million people visit Canada's capital every year. Here, a typical summer day on Sparks Street Mall, not far from Parliament Hill. Photo by Ari Tapiero.**

A strong sense of community
is fostered by participation in
our many festivals and special
events. Above, the Ottawa-
Carleton Police marching band
entertains the crowds.
Photo by Ari Tapiero.

Opposite page There is so much to
see and do! Here, a sunny atrium
beckons visitors inside to explore
the adjoining Currency Museum.
Photo by Ari Tapiero.

CHAPTER TWO

Capital History—
Legends, Glamour,
Politics & Intrigue

"*N*ear the mouth of this river is another coming

from the south, and at its mouth there is a

wonderful waterfall; for, from a height of 20 or 25

fathoms, it falls with such impetuosity that it

forms an archway nearly 400 yards in width.

The Indians, for the fun of it, pass underneath

this without getting wet, except for the spray made

by the falling water. There is an island in the

middle of this river, which, like all the land round

about, is covered with pines and white cedar."

—Samuel de Champlain

I n 1613, French explorer Samuel de Champlain was charting the route of the mighty Ottawa River, seeking a waterway that would allow fur traders safe passage through the wild, untamed lands of "New France." In his 10 years of exploration he had befriended the Algonquins and Hurons, two of the Indian tribes native to the area, and he had battled with the fierce Iroquois to establish the first permanent trading post at Quebec. Using a navigational aid known as an "astrolabe," Champlain's discoveries marked the beginnings of Canadian settlement, and his description of the Rideau River, where it meets with the Gatineau, is the first record of what we today recognize as Ottawa. Further up the Rideau, Champlain came upon a sacred ceremonial site and trading spot for the Algonquin tribe.

"At one place, the water falls with such force upon a rock that with the lapse of time it has hollowed out a wide, deep basin. Herein the water wheels around to such an extent, and in the middle sends up such big swirls, that the Indians call it *Asticou*, which means 'boiler.'" The French translation is *chaudiere*, and today we know this place as the Chaudiere Falls.

Little did the man who is remembered as the "Father of New France" know that along the banks of these rivers, the capital of a great country would grow. Nor could he realize that some 350 years after his death, his likeness would continue to survey these waterways. Champlain's statue towers high atop Nepean Point, not far from the Chaudiere Falls. His astrolabe was found over 250 years later in a farmer's field just west of Ottawa, and is today housed at the Canadian Museum of Civilization.

Fur traders and *couriers des bois* travelled the Ottawa River for the next hundred years, but the first real development of the Ottawa area wasn't established until the late 18th century. And although these first signs of industry occurred on the Quebec side of the river, it was not a French settlement, but an English one. By this time, the French had given up their rights to much of the lands they had discovered after being defeated by the British in a fierce battle at Montreal in 1760. Another battle, the American Revolution, marked the migration of the United Empire Loyalists to Upper Canada. Many of these British sympathizers were granted lands along the Ottawa River for their allegiance, while others, like lumber baron Philemon Wright, were seeking ways to make their fortunes and remain loyal to the King. Wright arrived at the banks of the Ottawa River near Chaudiere Falls on March 7, 1800, from Woburn, Massachusetts, and immediately saw the economic potential in the rushing rivers, tumbling waterfalls and virgin forests.

Over the next few years, Wright established sawmills, grist mills and tanneries, all powered by the waters of the Rideau River and the Chaudiere Falls, and named his settlement "Wrightsville." By 1826, farms, stores, a church and even a hotel had been established in the community on the river's north banks, which had grown to a population of 1,000. In 1875, the village was renamed Hull, after the township on the north side of the mighty Ottawa River.

On the south banks, where the city of Ottawa stands today, settlers were slowly moving across the new border to claim their land grants, and the British had plans to improve the water route from Ottawa to the town of Kingston, their military stronghold on Lake Ontario. These plans resulted in the historic Rideau Canal system, a marvel of engineering in its day which is still in use some 200 years later. The British planned to use the canal for military purposes; it would become a protected passageway for English naval forces and the transport of goods from the St. Lawrence River and Lake Ontario north to the Ottawa River, in the event of any further skirmishes with the Americans. The War of 1812, while a victory for the British, had pointed out their weaknesses in defending the natural border represented by the St. Lawrence River.

It was the construction of the 125-mile-long Rideau Canal that truly heralded the beginnings of today's Ottawa. The Rideau Canal was the life's work of Colonel John By, who was commissioned by the British government to direct some 2,000 men during the building of the canal's 47 locks– a process which began in 1826 and took six long, laborious years. Hundreds of workmen died in an outbreak of malaria in 1828, putting construction at a standstill for several weeks. But as tradesmen, labourers and their families moved into the area to build the great canal, a community grew, and they named their settlement "Bytown" in honour of the master engineer. Achieving city status in 1855, it was eventually renamed "Ottawa."

Around the time that the Rideau Canal work began, the first bridge spanning the river to link Wrightsville and Bytown was built—and the cities of Hull and Ottawa have been closely linked ever since. It was also in 1826 that the Byward Market was established. This traditional "farmers' market" is the oldest continuously operated market in Canada, and today remains a vital part of downtown Ottawa.

One of the tradesmen who was lured to the area by a masonry contract for the Rideau Canal left his mark with a home fit for a queen. Thomas McKay arrived in 1826 to work on the locks and decided to put down roots. This early entrepre-

neur went on to establish the McKay Milling Company, and his good fortunes translated into wealth. He directed his masons to build a grand "castle" in 1838, where he would live with his family. It was eventually purchased by the government as a home for the Queen's representative in Canada. Rideau Hall continues to house the Governor-General, even today, and is the official residence of British royalty when they visit the capital.

The first major political controversy in the nation's capital, strangely enough, took place over the selection of a capital city for the new "Province of Canada." Ottawa was not alone in

Opposite page **King George VI and Queen Elizabeth with Prime Minister Mackenzie King at Parliament Hill, circa 1939. Photo courtesy of the National Archives of Canada.**

Below **The traditional Changing of the Guard ceremony at Parliament Hill is a favourite with tourists during the summer months. Courtesy Canadian Tourism Commission.**

seeking this important designation. The growing city of Toronto, to the east, was under consideration. Kingston had held the honour in 1841; three years later, Montreal had been declared the seat of power, but riots resulted in the burning of Montreal's Parliament buildings. There was also, at that time, a certain rivalry between "Canada East" and "Canada West," and the decision-making process proved so difficult that Queen Victoria was asked to make the choice. There are two legends about how she ultimately selected the capital; some say she was intrigued by drawings of the area made by Lady Head, the wife of the Governor-General, while others claimed Her Majesty had simply closed her eyes and picked a spot on the map! Her method may remain a mystery, but Queen Victoria of England declared Ottawa as the capital of the "Province of Canada" on December 31, 1857. The Dominion of Canada, under Confederation, occurred a decade later.

Among the most visible legacies of the Queen's historic decision are the Gothic-style Parliament Buildings, influenced in part by their British counterpart, the Houses of Parliament in London, which had been built just a few years before. The future King Edward VII, then Albert Edward, Prince of Wales, laid the cornerstone for Ottawa's Parliament Buildings in 1860; it was the first royal visit to the capital. The great sandstone buildings with their copper roofs would take another five years to complete, partly due to the scope of the project and partly because costs at times exceeded funding. But the majestic buildings were, and remain, a home befitting government, although they were nearly lost in 1916, when fire swept through the House of Parliament, gutting the building and destroying the original Centre Block, the main tower crashing to the ground. The cause of the fire was never determined, although many said it was arson. The tall clock tower that stands as the centrepiece today is known as the Peace Tower. It was completed in 1927 and is dedicated to Canada's war heroes.

Fire was always a hazard in the Victorian era, and the two riverside communities suffered through many. One of the worst was known as the "Great Fire" of 1900. Seven people were killed and hundreds were left homeless. Sawmills, factories, public buildings—even the railway station—were destroyed or seriously damaged. But Ottawans were quick to rebuild, and many of the

capital's most famous landmarks arose after the fire, including the National Archives and the great stone fortress that houses the Royal Canadian Mint.

Another is the palatial Chateau Laurier Hotel, just next to Parliament Hill. The Grand Trunk Railway decided to build a French Gothic-style hotel and a new railway station, located across the street and connected by an underground tunnel. The hotel was named for then-Prime Minister Sir Wilfred Laurier, who had supported the railway system in general and the hotel project in particular. Construction began in 1907 and proceeded on schedule, in spite of some controversial cost-cutting measures by Charles Melville Hays, president of the Grand Trunk. But wherever he trimmed the budget, it could not be denied that the Chateau Laurier, with its 450 rooms, grand dining rooms and ballrooms and its stunning architectural design, was the most elegant and luxurious hotel many had ever seen. A grand opening gala was planned for April 26, 1912.

And then, tragedy struck. Charles Melville Hays was returning from a business trip to Britain with his wife, daughter, son-in-law and their servants. The return passage was to be an exciting one; the family was invited as guests of White Star chairman J. Bruce Ismay and would travel first class on the maiden voyage of the world's most famous ship—the *Titanic*. Hays' wife and daughter survived. The man responsible for Ottawa's grandest hotel did not. The Chateau Laurier quietly opened its doors on June 1, 1912. Sir Wilfred Laurier signed the register as the first guest.

In 1916, Canada's national agency for science and technological research was established in Ottawa. The National Research Council of Canada has made many significant contributions over the years, but its efforts during the Second World War made a major difference to the Allied Forces. Our experts contributed to the development of radar, allowing enemy vessels and planes to be spotted from a long distance. They designed portable refrigeration units for supply ships and invented a process to produce powdered eggs, both of which helped Great Britain when blocked supply routes prevented shipments of food. And a new method of producing metallic magnesium, a light metal alloy needed for fast fighter aircraft, was developed by NRC researchers.

The Second World War also marked the beginnings of another Ottawa tradition—the annual

Opposite page **The grandeur and elegance of the Chateau Laurier Hotel have made it a capital landmark. Courtesy Canadian Tourism Commission. Photo by Ted Grant.**

3

CHAPTER THREE

Capital Living—
A Place for All Seasons

*E*very season is a celebration in Ottawa,

a new opportunity to appreciate the beauty that

surrounds us in the National Capital Region.

The colours of our landscape change as the pages

of the calendar turn. We rejoice in the natural

palette of fall tones, as maple trees turn to crimson

and birches turn to a shimmering gold. And oh, to

be in Ottawa on a sparkling winter night, skating

on the frozen Rideau Canal or gliding down the

crisp snows of nearby Mont St. Marie!

*A*s spring warms the earth, millions of tulips come to life in an explosion of colour all across the city. And summer brings us hot, hazy days of sunbathing at the beach, sailing and boating on clean, clear waterways, fishing at one of the hundreds of freshwater lakes that dot the countryside, and cycling, camping and hiking through the rugged beauty of the Precambrian shield. In Ottawa, your senses come alive, all year round!

Ottawa is also a place for people of all ages, in all seasons of their lives. We're proud of our excellent education system; our schools are well-maintained and people oriented. The capital's universities and community colleges are producing graduates who are skilled not only in theory, but also in practice, ready for the workforce. And we boast a health care system that is the envy of the world. Our hospitals not only provide general care but specialized services as well, and are leading the way in medical research and treatment. Housing is affordable, whether it's in one of our award-winning new developments, an older, established neighbourhood or in one of the many heritage/condo restorations downtown. And we're pioneering the movement towards "child-friendly" cities, because we believe kids come first.

From recreation to education to health care and housing, Ottawa offers capital living every day of the year!

Ottawa—A Winter Wonderland

Hibernate? Far from it! The people of Ottawa revel in the splendour of white powder that blankets our city, and our wintertime is filled with activities. Our typical winter starts in mid-November and lasts through March with an average temperature of 22 degrees Fahrenheit. We bundle up with hats, mittens and scarves and take to the ice on the world's longest skating rink, the Rideau Canal—a focal point for winter fun throughout the season, and especially during our Winterlude Festival. Winterlude, which typically takes place over three weekends in February, is one of Canada's largest winter carnivals and draws over 600,000 visitors each year. You'll find works of art in the ice sculptures at Dow's Lake and Confederation Park, sleigh rides, toboggan hills and ice slides at the Children's Village and entertainment on various stages set up in the downtown area. It's not unusual to see entire families enjoying the fun on skates, and the best part is, most events are free!

We're also passionate skiers. There are seven ski resorts just minutes from downtown Ottawa. Cross-country ski enthusiasts can enjoy hundreds of kilometres of groomed trails, many of them in the beautiful 85,000 acres of natural wonders in Gatineau Park. Off the "beaten path," snowmobilers rendezvous at riverside restaurants along the Ottawa River after a day's exploration, and those with a more romantic side can cozy up in a horse-drawn sleigh, complete with jingling bells. And, naturally, you'll find thousands of kids (and adults) facing off at hockey rinks around the city—after all, it's practically our national sport.

Tulips—Our Harbinger of Spring

When Ottawa became a home away from home for the Dutch Royal Family, seeking protection during the Second World War, an annual celebration took root. Every spring, over 3 million tulips bloom across the city in a signature of spring—and it all began with a gift of 100,000 tulip bulbs from Holland. Today, our annual Tulip Festival is the largest in the world and draws thousands of visitors with live entertainment, special events and cultural celebrations at sites throughout the city.

Another sure sign of spring in the capital is "sugar time." There are several maple sugar bushes open to the public. History comes to life as schoolchildren watch the syrup-making process, from collecting sap from the trees to boiling the sweet syrup and serving it over fresh, hot pancakes. It's about as Canadian as you could imagine!

Hot Fun in the Summertime

Whether you're a sun worshipper, a fishing fanatic, a golf nut or tennis pro in the making, a leisurely stroller or a mountain biker, or you just like checking out the patio scene, Ottawa summers are ideal. We enjoy plenty of sunshine with an average temperature of 70 degrees Fahrenheit, and the warm weather also brings our local farmers back to the Byward Market to sell their fruits, vegetables and flowers in quaint, old-fashioned stalls. Colourful umbrellas mark the dozens of outdoor patios in the downtown area, and street musicians and entertainers known as "buskers" perform everything from classical music to magic shows, right on the sidewalks!

Opposite page, above **Maple trees yield the first taste of spring at dozens of sugar bushes near the capital. Courtesy Canadian Tourism Commission. Photo by Jim Merrithew.**

Opposite page, below **A peaceful summer evening on the Rideau River. The silhouette of Parliament Hill is a perfect backdrop for this group of rowing enthusiasts. Courtesy Canadian Tourism Commission. Photo by Deborah MacNeil.**

If you're at home on the water, the Rideau River system offers miles of waterways to explore, all the way to the Big Rideau Lakes, or you can head west up the Ottawa River to discover the charm of the Ottawa Valley. The Rockcliffe Yacht Club and the Britannia Yacht Club are located not far from downtown, while the Nepean Sailing Club at Andrew Haydon Park also gives access to the mighty Ottawa River. You'll see avid anglers dangling their lines over a bridge or from a bass boat on any of the hundreds of lakes and rivers within a 100-kilometre radius of the capital. Summertime is also perfect for hanging out at the beach. Mooney's Bay and Britannia Beach are the largest, but you'll find others along the banks of the Ottawa River as well. And, for the brave-hearted, there are several white-water rafting companies within an hour's drive of the capital.

Cycling is a way of life for many Ottawans. There are over 150 kilometres of cycling paths winding their way throughout parks and along the waterways. In fact, we've been named one of the top-10 "Best Cities" in the world for cycling by *Bicycling Magazine*. Across the river, Gatineau Park offers not only biking paths, but also spectacular challenges for mountain bikers. And, in the summer, over 25 kilometres of city streets are closed to automobile traffic on Sundays, allowing cyclists and rollerbladers to enjoy the scenic Ottawa River Parkway.

Love being out on "the links"? We have no fewer than 23 golf courses to choose from. Tennis players will find court time on one of 135 tennis courts in the capital. Equestrians will find a variety of clubs to pursue their sport, and the Rideau Carleton Raceway, open from April to December, offers the thrills of harness racing. Motor sports fanatics can "rev it up" at the Capital City Speedway, with stock car racing through the summer months.

Fall Festivities

As autumn approaches, the farming communities in the surrounding Ottawa Valley begin to reap their harvests and celebrate with fall fairs and festivals. From Arnprior to Killaloe, from

Opposite page **Among the world's largest winter festivals is the capital's own "Winterlude," which attracts more than 600,000 visitors each year. Here, the Rideau Canal is transformed into the world's longest skating rink! Courtesy Canadian Tourism Commission. Photo by Bruce Paton.**

Autumn is a kaleidoscope of colour in the capital. Here, cyclists enjoy the tranquillity of nearby Gatineau Park. Courtesy Canadian Tourism Commission. Photo by Ari Tapiero

Smith Falls to Perth, many of these communities were settled by the Scots and Irish, and traditions have been passed down through generations. Step dancers jig to the sounds of fiddle music as the valley towns celebrate another good year; "city folk" are always welcome, too!

Photographers, artists and nature lovers find autumn in the capital to be a breathtaking display of colour and texture. Ottawa is surrounded by rich forests, and fall is the perfect time to walk or cycle on our many nature trails in and around the city. And we often enjoy one last "heat wave" during October, where jackets are shed and sunglasses donned.

Year-Round Recreation

We're a "fit" city, and we have the recreational facilities to prove it. Ottawa has 6 major sports complexes, 17 indoor pools, 27 indoor arenas for hockey and figure skating and hundreds of outdoor facilities, not to mention dozens of private health and fitness clubs, spas and 6 YM-YWCA locations. No wonder we've produced Olympic champions like figure skater Elizabeth Manley, synchronized swimmer Carolyn Waldo, relay gold medallist Glenroy Gilbert and rower Alison Korn!

Recreation also lends itself to hobbies and crafts. Ottawa hosts a number of large craft fairs throughout the year, giving local artisans an opportunity to profit from their projects. Clubs ranging from radio-controlled airplane buffs to the Twelfth Night Society, a historical social club devoted to the Tudor era, offer a creative outlet for hobbyists of all persuasions. And the capital has almost 50 community centres which provide recreational and meeting space for neighbourhood groups.

World-Class Health Care

Ottawa's superb health care facilities put families and individuals in skilled, professional hands. From general and teaching hospitals to specialized facilities like the Children's Hospital of Eastern Ontario, renowned for its excellent standards in paediatric medicine, our hospitals reach out into the community to provide extended care and treatment. Research at the Ottawa Civic Hospital has yielded life-saving results with the internationally respected University of Ottawa Heart Institute, and our Regional Cancer Centre is on the leading edge of research and treatment.

World-class sports and recreation facilities are available for athletes in Ottawa, whether amateur or professional, and many Olympic medallists call the capital home. Photo by Ari Tapiero.

We're tremendously proud of our education system. Ottawa has one of the most computer-literate populations in the country, and our schools make new technology available to students of all ages. Photo by Ari Tapiero.

Palliative care, psychiatric care and our facilities for the developmentally disabled are all kept to the highest standards, and our maternity wards and neonatal care units are among the best in the country. Ongoing partnerships with the University of Ottawa have helped to train our health care professionals to excellence in technical and personal skills.

Capital Education

Ottawa is justifiably proud of its education system. From pre-school to private school, from the elementary to the university level, our schools put people first, and we endeavour to use the technology that today's working environment demands. While all of our schools meet the provincial standard of at least one computer per ten students, many offer a higher ratio, helping to make us one of the most computer-literate communities in the country, with a high percentage of Internet users. Ottawa has over 230 elementary schools, more than 40 high schools (including one which offers an International Baccalaureate program) and 8 alternative schools. Private schools include the prestigious Ashbury College and

Elmwood School for Girls. Across the river, the Outaouais region has four school boards as well, offering French and English language instruction.

The University of Ottawa, founded in 1848, is the largest bilingual university in North America, with a population of 30,000 students, teaching and support staff. Specialized programs include law and medicine; the university partners with area teaching hospitals, and its research efforts include the respected University of Ottawa Heart Institute. The new School of Information Technology and Engineering works closely with our high-tech sector in research and placement opportunities. The main campus is located on Colonel By Avenue in the downtown core, but with its cooperative programmes from the region to Europe, Latin America and Africa, "U of O" truly has a global reach.

Carleton University, with its main campus on Bronson Avenue, was founded in 1942 and has grown to become a 62-hectare campus with 29 buildings and programs available in over 50 disciplines. Architecture, journalism, humanities, industrial design, engineering and social work are just a few of the undergraduate and graduate degree programs offered at Carleton. Typical annual enrollment is 20,000, including part-time students. Carleton University also contributes valuable research and offers joint programs in science and engineering with the University of Ottawa.

Algonquin College of Applied Arts and Technology, established in 1967, boasts a placement rate of over 82 per cent for graduates, in fields ranging from health care, business, high technology, journalism, interactive multimedia and graphic arts, and many more; over 140 programs are available. This community college also offers continuing education and distance education programs outside the capital. Students at both Algonquin College and Carleton University have access to free Internet services.

St. Paul's University offers training in religion, philosophy and humanities. The Outaouais region also has the Université de Québec á Hull and La Cité collégiale, which offer education in the French language.

Several private vocational and training institutes specialize in business, secretarial, and, most recently, in computer programming and network administration, partly as a result of increased local demand for skilled workers by our high-tech sector.

Learning is a life-long process, and the Ottawa-Carleton Learning Foundation promotes that concept with 35 programs and services. With the help of local educators and the business community, the OCLF provides breakfast programs, volunteers, fund-raising assistance and a computer recycling and networking program throughout the capital.

Literacy is a key component of our lifestyle; there are also over 20 public libraries available to Ottawa residents, and we have more bookstores per capita than any other city in Canada.

Home Bases

Whether you prefer new homes, heritage mansions or high-rise living, housing in Ottawa is affordable and as varied as the people who live here. Neighbourhoods such as Rockcliffe Park, New Edinburgh, Sandy Hill, the Glebe, Centretown and Somerset Heights were established before the turn of the century. But all throughout the city, you'll find grand old homes that have been lovingly restored, carefully pre-

served and, best of all, lived in! There's a trend towards the restoration and renovation of heritage buildings; many of these were schools and other public buildings which are being cleverly restructured into condominiums and loft-style apartments. And, in the suburbs, new developments have been planned wisely to encourage the development of not only new housing but also new communities, complete with parks, schools and plenty of greenspace. The average price for a home in Ottawa is $136,686 (1996), with starting prices as low as $75,000 for townhouse condominiums in parts of the city.

The "Child-Friendly" Capital

Ottawa is one of the first North American cities to make a dedicated move towards becoming "child-friendly." A special committee has been established to explore new ways of reaching out to youth. "Child and Youth Friendly Ottawa" offers a hospitality program to encourage business to appeal to young people, a youth volunteer coordinating service, an arts and literature group and a government advisory committee comprised of young people.

Our Junior Board of Trade, under the guidance of the Ottawa-Carleton Board of Trade, has an active and enthusiastic membership of young entrepreneurs, many of whom are already headed towards success.

We already boast a plethora of museums designed to appeal to the eyes of a child, most notably the Museum of Science and Technology with its hands-on exhibits, and the Museum of Nature with its huge dinosaur displays and living examples of insects from around the world. As well, the "Computers for Kids" programme initiated in the capital is now used nationwide, recycling surplus computer equipment from government and industry and bringing it into use in the classroom. A volunteer network called "Partners in Education" is linking schools to local businesses, and "Innovators in the Schools" lets kids learn first-hand about engineering, science and technology from professionals, right here at home. In Ottawa, we believe young people are our future, and we want our city to continue to be their home. ■

Following page, left **Ottawa has homes to suit every lifestyle, from condominiums to gracious estates; prices are competitive and new developments are flourishing. Photo by Ari Tapiero.**

Following page, right **The city is filled with charming neighbourhoods where shoppers can find bargains in colourful open-air markets. Photo by Ari Tapiero.**

Photo by Ari Tapiero

CHAPTER FOUR

Capital Sights— You Won't Believe Your Eyes!

*F*rom the towering spires of the Parliament

Buildings to the ultra-modern National Gallery of

Canada, Ottawa's successful blend of old and

new extends to our sights and attractions, which

bring millions of people to the capital every year.

With dozens of historic sites and monuments, nearly 30 museums, two vibrant waterways, a full range of guided and self-guided tours, enticing shopping areas, designer malls and quaint neighbourhoods, Ottawa continues to delight (and educate!) visitors of all ages with something for every interest. And, whether you choose to walk, drive, take a double-decker tour bus or cruise down the Rideau Canal and the Ottawa River on one of our tour boats, you're sure to see something to catch your eye and your imagination!

Without question, the image of Parliament Hill has become the instantly recognizable icon for Ottawa, for it is not only the focal point for our national government, it is also the city's most popular tourist attraction. It truly is a "must-see" on every visitor's itinerary! Perched on a high cliff bank over the Ottawa River, the grounds of Parliament Hill are dotted with memorials and statues of prime ministers, royalty and Canadian heroes. The "Centennial Flame" (marking the 100th anniversary of Canada's confederation in 1967) burns at the entrance of the walkway to the 190-foot-high Peace Tower, the centrepiece of Parliament Hill's Centre Block. At its peak, an enormous clock, reminiscent of London's Big Ben, peals the hours with the chiming of 53 bells. Inside the Centre Block is the Memorial Chamber, honouring Canadians who gave their lives in war, and the magnificent chambers of the Senate and the House of Commons, where the policies and laws of our country are still made today. Guided tours of the Centre Block are offered year-round, and include a visit to the circular 19th-century Library of Parliament, with its ornate wood carvings and domed roof. Visitors can also tour parts of the East Block, which dates from 1865. (The West Block is not open to the public.) Parliament Hill's Visitor Welcome Centre and the Infotent (open during the summer season) are the best places to begin your visit.

Seasonal activities on "the Hill" include the colourful pageantry of the Changing of the Guard ceremony each morning during the summer, where the Governor General's Foot Guards and the Canadian Grenadier Guards parade. Summer evenings feature a multimedia show in celebration of our culture and history, projected onto the sandstone face of the Parliament Buildings. Christmas Lights on Parliament Hill are dramati-cally lit in early December and create a glittering display of colour and light throughout the holiday season. And, naturally, the grounds of Parliament Hill are the setting for the country's largest gathering for our national holiday on Canada Day, July 1st, with a giant stage, performances by Canadian musicians and a spectacular fireworks display.

Canada's highest court is found just next to Parliament Hill. You can walk through the hallowed halls of the Supreme Court of Canada on a guided tour during the summer months. Also near Parliament Hill is Major's Hill Park, set in the centre of the downtown area and home to many musical events and festivals throughout the year. One of the most popular spots for panoramic views of the Parliament Buildings and the Ottawa River is Nepean Point, where a statue of explorer Samuel de Champlain towers over the cityscape.

Portions of the stately home of the Governor-General, Rideau Hall, are open to the public, and the magnificent grounds with their wrought-iron and pillar fencing are the site of summer lawn parties and winter skating for all to enjoy. Twenty-four Sussex Drive is the home of Canada's prime minister, and although there are no public tours, it's a popular stop on many sightseeing routes. You can, however, wander through the home of one of our former prime ministers—the nearby MacKenzie King Estate offers an inside look at the home of one of our most famous historical figures.

The Ottawa River and the Rideau Canal are an integral part of Ottawa's character. You can visit the meeting point of these historic waterways, located next to the Chateau Laurier Hotel, and watch as the historic gates are cranked open to take pleasure craft to the next level of our canal system in the canal locks. If you'd like to get out on the water, one of the best places to do so is at scenic Dow's Lake on the canal, where canoes and pedal boats are available for rental. Later, you can relax on the waterfront patios of Dow's Lake Pavillion, or take a stroll through the gardens at Dow's Lake—particularly stunning in the springtime, when the tulips are in bloom. For the active-minded, there are booths along the canal walkways where you can rent roller blades or bicycles by the day or by the hour, and in winter, skate and sleigh rentals make the canal accessible

Opposite page **Many of Canada's national museums are found in the capital area. Here, a traditional native village scene has been recreated inside the Canadian Museum of Civilization. Photo by Ari Tapiero.**

to everyone. You may even catch a glimpse of the Royal Swans, a gift from Queen Elizabeth II, which are released each spring on the Rideau River.

Ottawa's 29 museums house many of our national treasures—from priceless art works to one of the last remaining sections of the infamous Avro Arrow, the plane regarded to be "ahead of its time" and of which all records, blueprints and pieces were ordered destroyed in 1959.

The astonishing architecture of the National Gallery of Canada (designed by renowned architect Moshe Safdie) is, in itself, a work of art. The predominantly glass building contains not only Canadian collections, including works by the Group of Seven, but has also acquired works by such European and American masters as Van Gogh, Rembrandt, Monet and Warhol. The National Gallery also features exhibits on tour, which have included the works of Renoir and Picasso. The Ottawa Art Gallery spotlights artists from the region and also has an impressive collection of works by nationally known artists. For those with an "eye" for the visual arts, the Canadian Museum of Contemporary Photography also gives the human perspective of our world, and often, the photographers are on hand to explain their works.

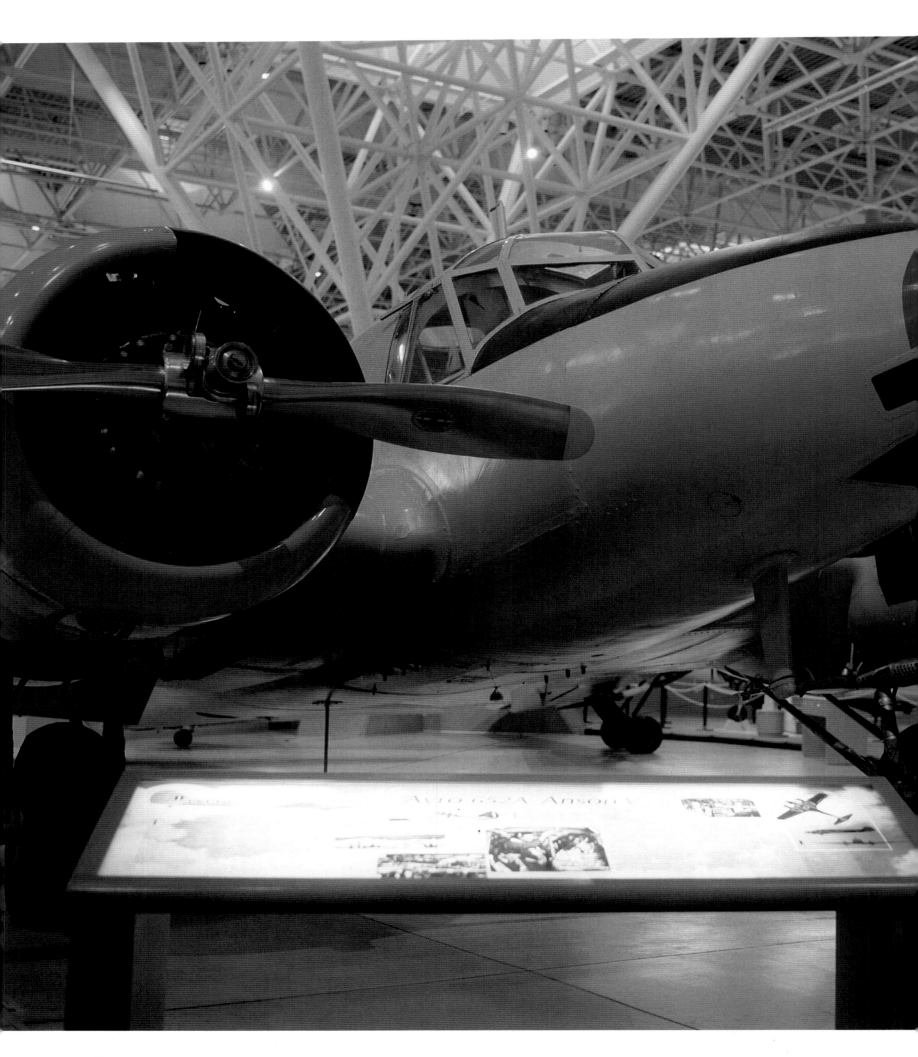

The Canadian Museum of Civilization is another architectural masterpiece. Designed by architect Douglas Cardinal, its graceful limestone curves are imbedded with fossils found in various parts of the country. This museum, with over 3.5 million artefacts in its permanent collection, is dedicated to Canadian history. You can see everything from re-enacted native villages and intricately carved totem poles to Champlain's astrolabe. The museum also features travelling exhibits from collections around the world. There is an interactive Children's Museum where youngsters can take a "tour" of the world, and two theatres featuring films in OMNIMAX and IMAX, which offer a new definition of the term "big screen"!

Science and technology are a part of daily life in Ottawa, and three of our museums bring science alive. You can walk amongst the dinosaurs at the Canadian Museum of Nature and see exhibits on Canadian wildlife, gems and minerals and artefacts from prehistoric times. The National Museum of Science and Technology gives visitors a chance to prove scientific theories with hands-on exhibits, from high-tech virtual reality to a huge collection of locomotives. And the National Aviation Museum, with over 120 military and civilian aircraft in its collection, pays tribute to Canada's aerospace and aviation pioneers. Permanent exhibits include the spacesuit of Canadian astronaut Marc Garneau and one of the last remaining pieces of the mysterious Avro Arrow interceptor aircraft.

Canadians have long been regarded as peacekeepers in troubled times, and the history of our military is preserved in the Canadian War Museum. Our National War Memorial in Confederation Square pays tribute to all Canadians who have served in war. As well, the country's only monument dedicated to peacekeepers is located across from Major's Hill Park, near Parliament Hill.

The imposing turrets of the Royal Canadian Mint are representative of the treasures this building holds. Canada's coins are still designed and engraved here, and gold, silver and platinum coins are minted inside the castle-like structure. Public tours are available. And money-lovers will also want to see the Currency Museum with the largest collection of Canadian coins and paper currency in the world.

The National Aviation Museum has over 120 vintage aircraft in its collection, including some of the last remaining pieces of the infamous Avro Arrow. Photo by Ari Tapiero.

Historical and literary treasures are found at the National Archives of Canada and the National Library of Canada, both open to the public. There are some 60 million records in the National Archives, including manuscripts, journals and photographs, while the National Library's collection includes thousands of Canadian publications, including rare and historical books.

Local history is preserved at the Bytown Museum, where you can learn more about the building of the Rideau Canal. Ottawa's oldest residential building, the Billings Estate, is also open to the public with its beautiful grounds and historical exhibits. And, for a glimpse into the history and the future of agriculture, visit the Central Experimental Farm, the largest research and working farm in the country. The barns are filled with dairy cows, sheep, pigs, horses and everything you'd expect to see "down on the farm." There's also a museum, exhibit area and children's playroom, and you can wander through the Arboretum and the greenhouses to see not only plants native to this region, but also specimens from around the world.

A Treasure Trove of Shops

Whether you're a bargain hunter, souvenir lover, antique collector, or you just appreciate quality merchandise, Ottawa has the kind of shopping you'll love. We have over 70 large shopping centres, including the Rideau Centre downtown, Bayshore Shopping Centre, St. Laurent Shopping Centre, Westgate Mall, Place d'Orleans and the Carlingwood Mall, and over 100 other smaller shopping centres to choose from. Or, if you prefer to stroll along the street and indulge in a little window shopping (and more!), try the Sparks Street Mall, the Bank Street Promenade, Somerset Village, Elgin Street or the Glebe for a myriad of shops and services. Ottawa also loves everything "old"! The Ottawa Antique Market is found on Bank Street and encompasses the wares of over 50 independent dealers, and several other antique shops can be found within just a few blocks.

Seeing It All

There are so many sights to see in Ottawa, and, to be sure you see them all, you may want to take one of the several guided tours available in the downtown area. One of the best routes by land is known as "Canada's Discovery Route."

Confederation Boulevard winds its way through the central part of downtown Ottawa and across the bridge to Quebec, with many of the largest sights and museums along the way, including Parliament Hill and the National Gallery of Canada.

You can get a bird's-eye view from one of the bright red double-decker buses operated by Capital Trolley Tours, with over 20 stops on its route where you can hop off and explore, and then ride on to the next site. Or, cruise down the Ottawa River or the Rideau Canal on one of the many boat tours available during the summer months from Paul's Boat Lines and the Ottawa Riverboat Company. Walking tours, both guided and self-guided, are plentiful and diverse, and for something completely different, take a ride on an authentic steam train! The H.C.W. Steam Train takes you on a journey through the valley of the Gatineau Hills to the town of Wakefield, Quebec. Or, you can take to the skies in a small aircraft or in a hot air balloon—several companies offer aerial sightseeing tours of the capital.

The National Capital Infocentre, operated by the National Capital Commission, is located directly across from Parliament Hill. Or, visit the Ottawa Tourism and Convention Authority at the National Arts Centre. Friendly and knowledgeable staff can guide you with information, brochures and directions to help you make the most of your sightseeing in the capital. ■

Opposite page **Elegant and modern, our major shopping centres continue to thrive as the retail sector in Ottawa flourishes. Photo by Ari Tapiero.**

Above **A strong sense of history surrounds us; here, a traditional gun salute on our national holiday, Canada Day. Courtesy Canadian Tourism Commission. Photo by Bob Anderson.**

Right **Kids (and parents!) love the Museum of Science and Technology, with exhibits ranging from vintage automobiles and steam trains to space technology and virtual reality. Photo by Ari Tapiero.**

Opposite page **At the Central Experimental Farm, the largest research and working farm in Canada, youngsters enjoy interacting with the barnyard residents. Photo by Ari Tapiero.**

CHAPTER FIVE

Capital Arts & Entertainment— Our World's a Stage!

"*W*hat would you like to do this evening?"

is a question well worth pondering here in

Ottawa, because the choices are so diverse!

The symphony, the opera, ballet, Broadway

shows and live theatre thrive here, alongside

big-league sports, high-rolling casino nights,

cutting-edge contemporary music and a myriad

of festivals and special events.

*O*ttawa is graced with a wealth of local talent, and also brings the most prestigious stars of the world's stages to its venues in a smorgasbord of arts and entertainment. International performers like Alanis Morissette, Rich Little, Paul Anka, Matthew Perry, Dan Ackroyd, Tom Cruise and many others have, at one time or another, called Ottawa "home," and found the roots of their talents carefully nurtured in our local arts and entertainment community. Today, hockey superstars like Alexei Yashin and Daniel Alfreddson live here, alongside budding musical talents like Suzie Vinnick and bluesman Tony D. And, not only do we have some of the world's best "players"—we have some of the world's best "stages"!

Front Row Centre

The newest addition to our offerings is the 18,500-seat Corel Centre, a world-class sports and entertainment facility which opened in 1996. Here, the NHL Ottawa Senators thrill crowds with nearly 50 home games each season, and play host to the best and brightest hockey stars. The $200-million Corel Centre is also the site of many other professional sporting events, such as the World Cup of Hockey, exhibition NBA basketball, national and international figure-skating competitions and has even hosted WWF wrestling, monster trucks and the rodeo! The Corel Centre is a favourite venue for performing artists, with close to 100 concerts and family shows each year. Bryan Adams, Celine Dion, Garth Brooks, the Eagles and scores of other top-name artists have already played the Corel Centre in the short time since it opened, and critics praise the acoustics and perfect sight lines the facility offers.

The prestigious National Arts Centre, with three separate stages, is the home of the National Arts Centre Orchestra and Ottawa's own Opera Lyra. Set along the banks of the Rideau Canal in the heart of downtown, the NAC is among Canada's premier showcase venues for the performing arts. The internationally acclaimed NAC Orchestra, founded in 1969, has featured guest artists such as Isaac Stern, Kathleen Battle and Itzak Perlman. Each year, the NAC hosts its dance series with troupes such as Les Grandes Ballets Canadiens, La La La Human Steps and the Toronto Dance Theatre. As well, the stages of the NAC host Broadway productions like *Cats* as well as performances by world-class artists ranging from Pavarotti to Anne Murray and Gordon Lightfoot, Bill Cosby, Bob Newhart and magician David Copperfield. Always active in the promotion of the arts, the NAC features a theatre series in both English and French, and premieres new works by Canadian playwrights throughout the year. Elegant and acoustically superb, the NAC is perfect for an evening soirée, and has an excellent restaurant, Le Café, with a summer canal-side terrace.

The Ottawa Symphony Orchestra, founded in 1965, performs a concert series each year at the NAC. The 90-member community symphony orchestra is comprised of freelance musicians, gifted amateurs and students from the various music programmes in the city, and auditions are held periodically. The Ottawa Symphony also performs at various other venues in the region.

The Ottawa Congress Centre is the site of several concerts throughout the year. Set in the heart of downtown, the Congress Centre has two separate venues for performers—the 3,500-seat Congress Hall and the 1,200-seat Capital Hall. Bob Hope, Diana Ross, B.B. King and Kenny Rogers are just a few of the stars who have graced its stages, and the Congress Centre always hosts one of the biggest New Year's Eve parties in the city.

The Great Canadian Theatre Company is a hotbed of burgeoning talent, with live theatre and musical performances throughout the year. Established in 1976, the 220-seat theatre features live drama as well as a musical series known as "Acoustic Waves," which has brought in well-known Canadian acts like Rita McNeil and Murray McLaughlin. The Nepean Centrepointe Theatre, in the city's west end, seats over 900 people and is the home of the Nepean Little Theatre, the Nepean Choir, Concert Band and Jazz Band, and the Orpheus Musical Theatre Society, which specializes in Broadway musicals. Centrepointe Theatre's stage also features world-class performers, such as the Moscow Philharmonic Orchestra, Lyle Lovett and Blue Rodeo, as well as comedy troupes, children's shows and cultural groups. Ottawa Little Theatre and the Kanata Theatre are among many other local drama groups in the capital region. And the Council for the Arts in Ottawa promotes the

Opposite page Ottawa's new Corel Centre has won praise from fans and critics alike. Home of our NHL Ottawa Senators, this versatile sports and entertainment facility also hosts world-class performers such as Celine Dion and Pavarotti in concert. Photo by Ari Tapiero.

Above **Music lovers will find no shortage of special events. Photo by Ari Tapiero.**

Right **Live theatre thrives in the capital. Here, a production at the National Arts Centre. © Rene Binet.**

advancement of the arts in the nation's capital with funding and facilities.

Nightlife

For an evening of glamour and excitement of a different nature, you can hop across the river to the fabulous new Casino de Hull, built in 1996 at a cost of $120 million. Open seven days (and nights!) a week, the stunning new waterfront Casino has 45 gaming tables and some 1,300 slot machines, with a breathtaking view of the Ottawa skyline from each of its two levels. There are also two restaurants and two lounges to choose from, and most of the major downtown hotels offer casino shuttle service.

Ottawa nightlife is legendary. There are well over 100 nightspots in the capital, from alternative and hiphop dance clubs to quiet jazz and blues clubs, rock 'n' roll emporiums and down-home country cabarets. Don't miss the capital's oldest and most famous nightclub, Barrymore's Music Hall, located in a restored 1914-style movie house. Artists like The Tragically Hip, U2, R.E.M. and Tina Turner have played here—it's Ottawa's answer to Toronto's infamous El Mocambo! Or visit the quirky Zaphod Beeblebrox, an alternative music club where Alanis Morissette and Cracker performed before hitting the international scene. Blues fans won't want to miss the venerable Rainbow in the Byward Market, and the best in stand-up comedy are on stage at Yuk Yuk's Comedy Cabaret.

The capital also has two Hard Rock Café locations (one at the Corel Centre, the other in the Byward Market), scores of British-style pubs like the Royal Oak, the Earl of Sussex and the Heart and Crown, and popular sports bars like Don Cherry's, Local Heroes and Marshy's Bar-BQ and Grill (owned by former NHL'er Brad Marsh and located at the Corel Centre).

Festivals and Seasonal Events

Ottawa hosts the country's largest birthday party each year on July 1st. Canada Day at Parliament Hill is a major celebration of national pride. Wellington Street, in front of the Parliament Buildings, is closed to traffic as hundreds of thousands of people gather at "the Hill" with lawn chairs and picnic baskets to enjoy performances by Canadian artists, and to see the spectacular fireworks display over the Peace Tower. As

Canada's capital, these celebrations are broadcast across the country, and activities spill over to various other sites in the downtown area, including Major's Hill Park and Confederation Square. It's the biggest party of the year!

Over half a million people flock to the capital each February to celebrate winter in a unique fashion. Winterlude, typically held during the first three weekends in February, is one of the largest festivals we celebrate in Ottawa. The Children's Village at Jacques Cartier Park features giant ice slides, hay rides, an outdoor food court and performances by children's artists. Our Rideau Canal is transformed into the world's longest skating rink with canal-side booths serving hot chocolate, maple sugar candy and our world-famous "Beavertails" (a fried pastry dusted with sugar). Ice sculptures are created with astonishing detail, music fills the air on the many stages set up in various areas downtown, and you can watch everything from a waiter/waitress race on skates to a hockey shoot-out with NHL stars.

Ottawa's other signature event is the annual Canadian Tulip Festival, a celebration of spring capped by the 3 million tulips in bloom across the city. The main site at Major's Hill Park features cultural performances, children's workshops and activities and a wonderful array of crafts by local artisans. The 11-day festival, held in May, also offers horticultural and floral displays, lectures and workshops. Established in the 1950s, it has grown to become the largest Tulip Festival in the world and celebrates an international theme, featuring a different country every year.

And, while Canada Day, Winterlude and the annual Canadian Tulip Festival are perhaps the largest seasonal events in the capital, the Ottawa area hosts many others throughout the year.

One of the most visually stunning is the Gatineau Hot Air Balloon Festival, which takes place in September. Hundreds of giant hot air balloons fill the skies of the region in an incredible display of colour. The National Capital Airshow is one of the largest in Canada and traditionally features a performance by the famous Canadian Forces Snowbirds. And, keep looking up—our International Fireworks Competition draws entrants from around the world in lighting up the nightscape with pyrotechnics, all set to music!

Music lovers will find no shortage of special events. Several locations downtown take part

Canada's own—The Tragically Hip
on tour in *Another Roadside
Attraction*. Photo by Ari Tapiero.

Canada's acrobatic aviators, the Snowbirds, are a favourite during the National Capital Air Show. Courtesy Canadian Tourism Commission.

CHAPTER SIX

Capital Culture—
A Global Community

"*C*ulture, the acquainting ourselves with the best

that has been known and said in the world, and

thus with the history of the human spirit."

—*Matthew Arnold*

*I*t is fair to say that there is no quintessential "Ottawan." Instead, here you'll find a blend of peoples who have brought their traditions, their religions, their skills and their imaginations to Canada's capital. From our aboriginal peoples and the descendants of the original English and French settlers to our international embassies and the influx of skilled workers to the region, the result is a diverse city that welcomes and respects the many cultures that define who we are. Perhaps the common quality we share in Ottawa is an appreciation of these differences, an admiration for each other's areas of wisdom, a desire to learn from one another, a respect for and celebration of our many cultures. We have become a global community, and it has made us strong.

Some people say that Ottawa has a "European flavour." This may be attributed, in part, to the early settlements of the French and English in the region—many here can trace their roots back to the United Empire Loyalists and the pioneers of Quebec. Today, our proximity to the province of Quebec has given many of us the opportunity to become fluent in both of Canada's official languages, and it's not unusual to hear conversations that shift from one language to another with laughter and ease.

But that "European flavour" has been greatly enhanced by the contributions of our citizens who have come from countries all over the world, and who have found Ottawa a place to call home. As Canada's capital city, Ottawa has over 100 foreign embassies, consulates and high commissions, including those of the United States, Japan, Israel, India, Switzerland, France, Britain, Spain, Germany, Mexico—virtually every major player in the global economy. In these "homes away from home," representatives from many cultural backgrounds have found Ottawa to be a world-class city which welcomes and respects people from all parts of the globe.

Cultural Events

Celebrations of our many cultural components are opportunities to learn through music, dance, art and, of course, food! Each year, Ottawa hosts dozens of cultural festivals. One of the newest is the Carnival of Cultures, which brings together people of all countries just before our national holiday, Canada Day. Festival Franco-Ontarien is

usually held in June. This four-day outdoor celebration includes concerts, buskers, a café and a market area where artisans and craftspeople offer their creations. Féte-Caribe is a week-long celebration during the summer at various sites in the downtown area. It kicks off with a colourful (and noisy!) parade and features a boat cruise, children's area, music and dance, as well as crafts and great food. Ottawa's Preston Street is closed to traffic during Italian Week celebrations, and giant flags adorn the shops and restaurants in our "Little Italy." The doors are flung open, outdoor grills and patio tables are brought out into the street, and you can wander down the block to enjoy music, dancing, films and much more. The annual Greek Festival is held each summer at the Hellenic Community Centre. Everyone can join in the traditional Greek dances (you might even get to break the plates!) and shouts of *"Opa!"* (a Greek toast) fill the air. The giant outdoor dining area serves up *souvlaki*, spit-roasted lamb, Greek salad, *spanikopita* and *dolmades*, while indoors, you can wander through exhibits of art and traditional clothing. The Latin American Festival, the Philippines Festival, the German Festival and Lebanese Week are just a sampling of the other cultural events we celebrate during the year. And Ottawa's native community hosts the annual Odawa Powwow each spring, where thousands turn out to see colourful costumes, aboriginal dancing and drum ceremonies.

The needs of a wide variety of cultures are served by individual cultural groups and by the non-profit Multicultural Centre. As well, the Ottawa Multicultural Folk Arts Council provides support and meeting space to over 60 community and arts-related groups in the city.

In Praise of Our Differences

Places of worship in Ottawa number over 350 and include synagogues, mosques and temples, as well as churches and cathedrals. Ecumenical services are held at various locations throughout the year, and people of all faiths can join together to celebrate life.

Ottawa's Jewish community is the second-fastest growing in Canada, with over 12,000 members at six synagogues in the capital region. The Jewish Community Centre of Ottawa offers recreational facilities, community programmes and day care, along with a day school for children

Opposite page **The sharing of cultural traditions gives our community a rich view of the world. Photo by Ari Tapiero.**

up to grade eight and high school programmes for youth. Plans call for an expansion of these facilities to a large campus complex with a senior citizens' home.

The Catholic community also takes an active role, with over 75 churches and several community outreach programmes, including Catholic Family Services and the Catholic Immigration Centre, dedicated to helping newcomers settle

into a new life in Canada. Ottawa also offers a Catholic school system, with education from the primary to the high school level.

The Anglican church offers social services including counselling and health care, and offers day programmes in addition to operating two women's crisis centres. There are 54 Anglican churches with some 21,500 members in Ottawa. There are also large and active communities

Almost everywhere you look, you'll find a cultural experience in the making. Photo by Ari Tapiero.

Ottawa loves to lend a helping hand. Pictured here is one of our more unusual charity events, the annual "Duck Race" for the Children's Hospital. Photo by Ari Tapiero.

within the Presbyterian, Lutheran, Pentecostal, Baptist and Mormon faiths, as well as nearly 50 United churches in the region.

Helping Hands

Another unique aspect of Ottawa culture is the remarkable generosity and spirit of community demonstrated by the people who live here. From corporate donations by the area's high-tech industry to bottle drives and food collections by Ottawa area school children, the capital raises millions of dollars for charity each year. Some of the biggest events include the annual CHEO Telethon for the Children's Hospital of Eastern Ontario, the Ottawa Heart Institute Telethon to raise funds for continuing research in the capital, the annual Terry Fox Run for cancer research and the Tour des Quickies, a bicycle marathon which

raises money for area hospitals. Each spring, nearly 100,000 yellow rubber ducks are released into the Rideau Canal in the Kiwanis CHEO Duck Race, a fun and unusual fund-raiser for the Children's Hospital.

Virtually all well-known charitable organizations have an Ottawa chapter and are active in our community, including the Variety Club, the United Way/Centreaide, the Boys and Girls Club and Big Brothers/Big Sisters. You can also become involved in a number of service clubs, such as the Kiwanis, Kinsmen, Lion's Club and the Rotary Club, to name a few.

Mass Media

Ottawa prides itself on being a well-informed and well-educated community, and our media play an important role in educating the public. As

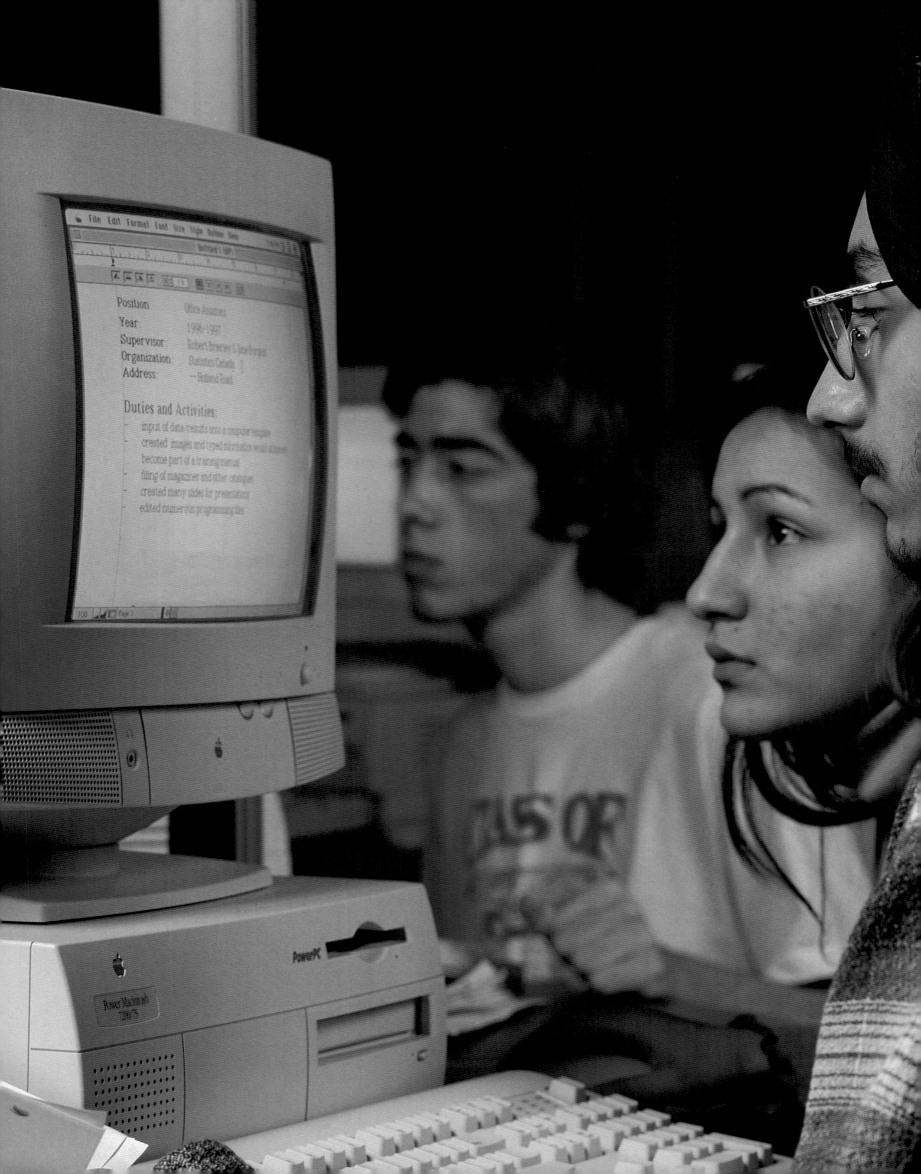

the nation's capital, journalists from media outlets around the world are represented here in Ottawa, and our local media are among the most well respected in the country. The capital has two large English-language daily newspapers—the *Ottawa Citizen* and the *Ottawa Sun*—and a French-language daily, *Le Droit.* There are also over 50 community newspapers and independent journals, including *Ottawa X Press*, a weekly entertainment publication, and the alternative lifestyle newspaper, *Capital Xtra.* Business publications include the *Ottawa Business Journal,* the *Ottawa Transcript* and *Silicon Valley North,* focusing on the high-tech industry. Each month, Capital Publishers puts out an informative tourism and events booklet, *Where,* and the prestigious *Ottawa Magazine* brings you political commentary, profiles of business leaders, lifestyles and entertainment news and more in a full-colour glossy publication.

We also have three award-winning local television stations serving an audience of over 2.5 million viewers. CBOT is Ottawa's bureau of the Canadian Broadcasting Corporation and produces local programs as well as news and entertainment programming for national broadcast. CJOH-TV, owned by Baton Broadcasting, is an affiliate of the CTV national network, which also provides local programming, and is renowned for its excellent news coverage and community involvement. CHRO-TV offers local programming as well, with a focus on communities in the Ottawa Valley. There is also our community channel—Rogers Community Cable—which gives people from all walks of life the opportunity to create and participate in local television productions. There are also nearly 40 cable and specialty channels available for viewers.

The capital also boasts 16 English-language radio stations, ranging from country music to rock 'n' roll, contemporary and classical. Both Carleton University and the University of Ottawa operate campus radio stations which broadcast throughout the city.

A "Connected" Community

Ottawa has been a pioneering force in the new information age with our strong high-tech sector, and that strength has translated to a computer-literate society. A large proportion of our population (65 per cent in an independent poll) has a personal computer in their homes—over twice the

Ottawa's computer literacy rate is well above the national average. Photo by Ari Tapiero.

national average. And one-quarter of those are "on-line" with Internet service, compared to just 7 per cent across Canada in the same poll. Our National Capital Freenet is one of the largest freenets in the world, with over 60,000 members. Headquartered at Carleton University and sponsored by the local business and high-tech community, the National Capital Freenet was one of the first to be established in Canada and has evolved to become an integral part of communications both in and from the capital.

Interest in the Internet is on the rise in the capital, and you'll find hundreds of Ottawa-area Web pages to browse through, including tourism sites and business links like the Ottawa-Carleton Board of Trade, the Ottawa-Carleton Research Institute, the Ottawa-Carleton Economic Development Corporation and the Regional Municipality of Ottawa-Carleton—and that's just a brief sampling!

A Perfect Fit

With an open-door policy, a forward-thinking population and an appreciation for the unique traits and contributions of our citizens, Ottawa makes room for everyone. Our blend of cultures is one of our hallmarks—one that we are immensely proud of. We roll out the red carpet for newcomers to the capital and welcome them into the fold, while allowing individuality to shine and prosper. In the capital, we think you'll find a perfect fit! ■

There are many cultural festivals throughout the year which celebrate our diversity. Here, tradition lives on at the annual Odawa Powwow. Photo by Ari Tapiero.

**Ottawa offers an environment
which encourages creativity.
Photos by Ari Tapiero.**

CHAPTER SEVEN

Capital Hosts—
Be Our Guest!

*W*e're justifiably proud of our international

reputation as "capital hosts," as over 5 million

people visit Ottawa every year! Tourism is among

our largest industries; visitors spend over 600

million dollars annually and help to generate

over 12,000 full-time jobs in our hospitality sector.

But here in the capital, we value not only the

economic impact, but also the friendships

we forge and the experiences we enjoy with

our guests from around the world.

*T*he Ottawa Tourism and Convention Authority and the National Capital Commission are dedicated to making your visit to the capital a success. We're rapidly becoming one of the preferred destinations in North America for both business and pleasure. Ottawa hosts literally hundreds of conferences and conventions each year. Our meeting and convention facilities are modern, functional and diverse, and the capital region has over 9,000 hotel rooms available for visitors. You'll have ready access to the many professional conference and meeting planners in the region who can not only take care of the arrangements and catering for you, but can also provide simultaneous translation services, video conferencing and multimedia displays.

And with our international airport, rail service and transportation links, Ottawa is so accessible! Montreal, Toronto, New York City, Washington, D.C.—all are just a quick flight, ride or drive away, making the capital a convenient site for your next major business function—so you, too, can be a "capital host."

Getting Here—From Anywhere!

With the recent Open Skies agreement and improved facilities and services, getting to Ottawa is a breeze. Our newly privatized Ottawa International Airport, officially known as Ottawa Macdonald-Cartier International Airport Authority, has increased the number of U.S. and domestic flights to and from the capital, and has added convenient pre-clearance facilities and extended hours for U.S. Customs and Immigration as part of an $8-million expansion plan for 1997. Over 16 airlines, including carriers like Air Canada, Canadian Airlines International, American Airlines, Delta and USAir offer direct and connecting flights to most major U.S. cities and access to the world. A new state-of-the-art air traffic control tower and radar room opened in 1992, and the terminal itself is modern, spacious and easy to get around. Serving nearly 2.5 million travellers each year, Ottawa International is Canada's fifth-busiest airport; the number of international passengers has increased by nearly 55 per cent in the past two years. And the four-lane Airport Parkway brings travellers downtown in about 15 minutes!

Smaller commuter and cargo aircraft can also touch down at the Carp Airport, just minutes

away from Silicon Valley North. This regionally owned airport was recently privatized after a $2-million renovation project and handles a significant number of business flights for the capital's high-tech center. A pre-registration customs clearance system known as "Canpass" speeds up cross-border travel. Carp Airport is a major base for high-tech shipments and also provides helicopter services as well as facilities for privately owned aircraft.

VIA Rail offers passenger train service with frequent daily departures through the Montreal-Toronto-Windsor corridor, as well as other destinations in Canada and connections to the United States. The VIA Rail Station is centrally located, just minutes from downtown.

Ottawa is a short drive from two other major Canadian cities. To the east, Montreal is about two hours away by car or bus, and to the southwest, Toronto is just a 400-kilometre trip. Several other cities, such as Kingston and Brockville, are nearby, and the U.S. border at New York is less than an hour's drive from the capital.

Destination Ottawa—Our Tourism Organizations

The capital's success as an international tourism destination is no accident. Two major organizations have played a large part in "putting us on the map," and continue to offer a helpful and welcoming hand to travellers.

Since 1971, the Ottawa Tourism and Convention Authority has been providing tourism information, assistance in conference and convention planning in the capital and a network of promotional and marketing opportunities to its 400 members. OTCA produces informative maps, visitors' guides, brochures and destination planning guides for worldwide distribution. It also encourages conventions and group tours as well as general tourism through its hosting programs and services. Working closely with the National Capital Commission, OTCA operates a toll-free visitors' information and reservation line which can be accessed from anywhere in North America. The OTCA's Internet Web site also provides a wealth of information on activities, attractions and accommodations in the area.

The National Capital Commission has a broad mandate which includes providing tourism information to capital visitors as well as organizing and promoting major events like Canada Day

Opposite page **Millions of people visit Canada's capital each year. Our road, rail and air connections have made Ottawa easily accessible from around the world. Photo by Ari Tapiero.**

The National Capital InfoCentre is conveniently located across from Parliament Hill, in the heart of the downtown core. Photo by Ari Tapiero.

on Parliament Hill and our annual Winterlude Festival. It's also responsible for much of the "greenspace" we enjoy here; parks, recreational pathways and wilderness areas are protected by the NCC. The newly opened Capital InfoCentre, across from Parliament Hill, is the main source of tourism information services and is staffed by friendly and knowledgeable guides who can provide everything from simple maps and brochures to a hotel reservation. During the summer months, an additional tourist information center, the Capital InfoTent, is set up on the grounds of Parliament Hill.

Ottawa's Hotels—So Accommodating!

With many hotels and motels and several quaint bed and breakfasts, Ottawa offers plenty of choice in terms of ambiance, budget and taste. Many of our major hotels have won international awards for quality and service; they're part of the

reason that so many visitors to Ottawa return again and again.

The historic Chateau Laurier Hotel is a capital landmark. This palatial hotel has 425 rooms, with suites offering an impressive view of the nearby Parliament Buildings and the Rideau Canal. The Chateau Laurier has retained the charm of days gone by and continues its tradition of gentility; a traditional afternoon tea in the British style is still served daily. Two upscale restaurants, a cozy piano bar and an outdoor terrace offer tempting menu choices. With 4 ballrooms and 16 banquet and meeting rooms, the Chateau Laurier is a popular site for weddings, soirées and business functions.

The downtown Westin Hotel, with 484 rooms and executive suites, offers the capital's largest ballroom with another 13 meeting and banquet rooms of various sizes. With a stunning view of Ottawa's skyline, the Westin has a convenient indoor connection to both the Rideau Centre and the Ottawa Congress Centre and features 2 restaurants, a lounge and a health club.

Not far from Parliament Hill, the Citadel Ottawa Hotel and Convention Centre has been newly renovated and, with 26,000 square feet of meeting space, can host functions of all types and sizes. Over 400 rooms, along with 22 suites, are available, as well as a health club, restaurant and lounge.

The Sheraton Ottawa Hotel and Towers is also set in the capital's downtown area. Part of the ITT Sheraton chain, the Sheraton Ottawa offers a Business Centre, an executive boardroom, 8 meeting rooms and a full penthouse conference

center with a stunning panorama of the city. Over 235 rooms, some on the exclusive Towers Level, as well as a fitness center and indoor pool round out the Sheraton's amenities.

The Radisson Hotel Ottawa Centre is another part of Ottawa's downtown skyline, with a revolving rooftop restaurant, a café and lounge, fitness facilities and nearly 500 rooms and suites. Executives can choose to stay on one of two business-class floors, and the Radisson also provides over 26,000 square feet of function space, including a 6,460-square-foot ballroom for larger events. The Radisson provides direct access to a complex of shops and services known as Place de Ville.

The historic Chateau Laurier Hotel retains the stately elegance of bygone days. Photo by Ari Tapiero.

Another choice for those who like to be in the heart of downtown is the Delta Ottawa Hotel & Suites. Just next to the Sparks Street Pedestrian Mall and a few blocks from Parliament Hill, the Delta's 329 rooms include over 60 suites. The Delta offers a business lounge and boardroom, along with banquet and meeting space for groups of up to 300. The hotel also features 2 restaurants and a health club, with a 115-foot indoor water slide.

Travellers with a penchant for the "suite life" will find just that at four capital hotels that specialize in this type of accommodation. The Minto Place Suite Hotel has over 400 studios, one- and two-bedroom suites and is close to "the Hill" and other downtown attractions. It's also attached to Minto Place, with 25 shops and services (including restaurants and a health club) and two office towers. Minto Place Suite Hotel features boardroom suites for small business meetings, 11 other banquet and meeting rooms and a large boardroom with a cityscape view.

Les Suites Hotel is just steps from the Rideau Centre and the Ottawa Congress Centre, with over 240 one- and two-bedroom suites to choose from. Les Suites has a café and health club as well as 3 additional meeting rooms.

The Albert at Bay Suite Hotel is also right downtown and offers nearly 200 suites, 3 meeting rooms, a bistro-style restaurant and a 24-hour convenience store. And the Best Western Victoria Park Suites has 100 suites available with a penthouse fitness club and access to meeting facilities.

Built at the turn of the century, the Lord Elgin Hotel is another traditional Ottawa landmark with its copper roofs and stately architecture. Just across from Confederation Park, the Lord Elgin provides 300 guest rooms and 11 meeting rooms, with a galleria-style restaurant and a lounge.

The Novotel Ottawa Hotel is located on Nicholas Street, one of the capital's main downtown thoroughfares, with 283 rooms and 15 suites available to travellers. The Novotel has 8 board-

room suites and 5 additional banquet and meeting spaces, and offers a health center, a bistro and a lounge for relaxation.

The Ramada Hotel and Suites is part of the North American chain so familiar to many. In Ottawa, the Ramada offers 235 guest rooms and suites with a restaurant, fitness center and 7 banquet and meeting rooms.

Other major hotels you'll find in the downtown area include the Market Square Inn, the Capital Hill Hotel & Suites, the Business Inn, the Travelodge Hotel by Parliament Hill, the Embassy Hotel & Suites, the Quality Hotel, the Super 8 Hotel Ottawa, Cartier Place & Towers Suite Hotel, the Days Inn Ottawa City Centre and the Howard Johnson Plaza Hotel.

Towards the west, the Best Western Macies Hotel, The Embassy West Motor Hotel, the Talisman, The Luxor Hotel, the Best Western Barons Hotel, and the Comfort Inn Kanata offer quick access to Silicon Valley North. Chimo Hotels Ottawa is located in the city's eastern section, as is the Ottawa East TravelLodge. Close to the airport, you'll find the Southway Inn, the Monterey Inn and Adam's Airport Inn.

For bed and breakfast lovers, there are dozens of independent establishments nearby, such as the historic Sam Jakes Inn and Strathmere House, which offer a home-like atmosphere for business travellers and tourists alike.

Conference and Convention Facilities— Designed to Impress

In addition to the meeting spaces offered by the capital's major hotels, Ottawa boasts several other large venues for trade shows, conventions and conferences.

The Corel Centre, with 22,000 square feet of exhibit space on its arena floor, is becoming a popular site for large business shows and gatherings. This multimillion-dollar sports and entertainment complex is conveniently located near many of the region's high-tech companies and also has up to eight meeting and banquet rooms available. These can range in size to suit specific requirements up to 7,350 square feet. Professional catering as well as audio-visual requirements can be arranged, and there are also three restaurants within the Corel Centre that are accessible to delegates and conventioneers. Many choose to combine their business functions with

Some of the world's top chefs are found in the capital, and our restaurants feature cuisine from around the world. Pictured here is Le Café at the National Arts Centre, where you can dine alongside the beautiful Rideau Canal. Photo by Ari Tapiero.

an "after hours" event like a hockey game or concert; the Corel Centre offers attractive options for business entertaining, including nearly 140 corporate suites and upscale "club seat" service.

The Ottawa Congress Centre has a long history of successfully run business events. Just next to the beautiful Rideau Canal, the 84,000-square-foot Congress Centre can host functions of all sizes, from small gatherings to conventions of up to 5,000 delegates, with full catering, translation booths and customized set-ups. Modern design on all four levels and a close-up view of the capital's downtown area add a sophisticated air. The Congress Hall level measures nearly 67,000 square feet and is sub-dividable, with access to the Rideau Centre and the Westin Hotel. The Capital Hall level provides another 12,500 square feet with a variety of set-ups ideal for seminars. The Colonel By Salon and other smaller meeting rooms are perfect for intimate gatherings. You can even arrange for an outdoor terrace reception, complete with a canopy tent.

Lansdowne Park and the Ottawa Civic Centre are traditional sites for trade and consumer shows, with venues ranging from the 10,500-seat Civic Centre arena to the 30,000-seat outdoor Frank Clair Stadium. Over 33,000 square feet of indoor space is available, including the historic Aberdeen Pavilion, which was recently restored to its turn-of-the-century splendor.

And many of our popular attractions also have conference and meeting capabilities. The National Arts Centre provides an elegant backdrop for business gatherings with four meeting rooms, the largest nearly 5,000 square feet. Dow's Lake Pavilion, with its stunning waterfront setting, has meeting space for up to 120 people. The Canadian Museum of Civilization and the National Gallery both offer banquet and reception rooms, while the Canadian Museum of Nature has seven separate rooms for smaller business functions.

The government's Conference Centre, across from the Chateau Laurier Hotel, was originally the capital's main passenger railway station. Built during the same period, the imposing limestone building now functions as the prime center for government conferences and meetings.

The University of Ottawa, Carleton University and Algonquin College also offer space for professional gatherings, and arrangements can often be made for dormitory accommodations during the summer months.

Capital Cuisine

Our rich cultural blend has had another spin-off effect; Ottawa restaurants feature the cuisine of the world, and the menu of choices seems endless. We have over 1,500 restaurants, from haute cuisine to contemporary, from Afghan to Vietnamese, and everything in between! Capital chefs often bring home medals from the Culinary Olympics in Frankfurt, Germany. Canadian and New World cuisine are on the cutting edge of creativity here; traditional French and Italian restaurants are highly rated as well. Casual dining ranges from steak and seafood to fondue cellars, Cajun/Creole and 1950s-style diners. Whether you're dining on an outdoor terrace along the Rideau Canal, in an elegant formal dining room amid crystal and chandeliers or on a bustling patio in the Byward Market, you're sure to discover a restaurant to suit your individual taste.

Throughout the year, we also offer a variety of food festivals, such as A Taste of Ottawa and the Ottawa Food and Wine Show, as well as more casual events, including an annual chicken and rib cook-off which draws participants from across North America.

From our luxury hotels and gourmet restaurants to our bed and breakfast inns and small, family-run cafés, the level of service and hospitality you'll find in Ottawa is consistently superb—and it's straight from the heart. We love our city, and we want to share it with you. ■

You'll find many of your favourite spots in Ottawa, such as the world-famous Hard Rock Café. Photo by Ari Tapiero.

"Down-home barbeque" comes to the Sparks Street Mall each summer during our annual chicken and rib cook-off. Photo by Ari Tapiero.

CHAPTER EIGHT

Capital Business Connections— On Track with Trade

*W*elcome to the global market! Companies located in Ottawa are recognized around the world, and a big part of that success lies in the hospitable business atmosphere we've created. We're competitive both at home and abroad. The spirit of cooperation and the commitment to the continued development of business growth here in the capital open the doors to profit through strategic alliances, shared knowledge and a strong and unified voice–a voice that is now being clearly heard in markets around the world.

"*B*usiness connections" brings to mind another connotation—one of accessibility and strategic location. As the nation's capital, Ottawa is home to the federal government and its departments involved in economic development and trade, customs, research, grants and procurements. Those resources are virtually in our backyard!

Strength in Numbers—Networking in the Capital

Whether it's high technology, life sciences, manufacturing, tourism, consulting or retail, Ottawa's thriving entrepreneurial sector keeps its finger on the pulse of new trends and opportunities by networking. The sharing of our resources and hearty support from existing businesses towards new ventures are a source of pride here; it's a "let's pull together" atmosphere. There is nowhere better to be in terms of research and development and the sharing of resources and information. The organizations you're about to discover not only work independently, but also cooperatively, on many projects. In Ottawa, we believe there is strength in numbers, and we work together to create and maintain a sustainable, vibrant and diverse economy. The roots of that goal are already firmly entrenched here, and there is only one way to go—up!

The Ottawa-Carleton Board of Trade plays a leading role in that network of support. As the Chamber of Commerce for Ottawa-Carleton, it is the voice of the capital's business community. The Board of Trade has successfully lobbied for change to help create the healthy business climate we enjoy in the capital today. Now in its 140th year, the Board of Trade has historically been a forward-thinking association geared to monitoring trade and government in our region and to exploring new ways to develop our private sector. Today, it continues to take a stand on issues impacting local business, whether it is change to government policies, strategies to improve transportation links or drumming up support for local business initiatives. Its mission is to make doing business in and from Ottawa a profitable proposition, with a diverse economic base on which to build our future. The Board of Trade favours a team approach between business and government to achieve these shared goals and stays in tune with its 1,500 members via specialized committees and regular surveys to identify and monitor the changing needs of our business community.

With a hands-on approach, the Board of Trade is also one of the premier networking alliances in the capital. It provides over 100 events and activities each year. These include not only regular seminars on a wide range of topics relevant to business, but also the chance to network through more informal gatherings. Events such as the monthly Board of Trade Civic Luncheon, "Breakfast Connections," and "Business After Hours" open the doors to making new business contacts, and help to keep members informed about new developments in Ottawa-based business and industry which may lead to spin-off opportunities and increased profits.

The Board of Trade also plays an important role in "getting the word out" about our hundreds of local success stories. It hosts the annual Ottawa-Carleton Business Achievement Awards, a regular Business Showcase event, and is instrumental in managing a series of business stories known as the "Good News Network," regularly carried by local media.

The Ottawa-Carleton Economic Development Corporation (OCEDCO) encourages business location and expansion in the capital through a number of initiatives, and plays a leading role in marketing our region to the world. OCEDCO will assist in everything from helping you to select a site for your business in the capital to facilitating opportunities for alliances and trade. OCEDCO has the "hard numbers" businesses need in their decision-making processes, from industrial land costs to average taxes and operating costs. They also help to match businesses with venture capital and track investment opportunities.

OCEDCO is also an important resource for small business in Ottawa. Small businesses can take advantage of the expertise of the Entrepreneurship Centre. It is funded by the region's government, as well as by the province of Ontario. Each year, over 40,000 clients take advantage of the services, seminars and information offered by the Entrepreneurship Centre, and more than 375 new business starts in 1996 alone were the result of these efforts, representing millions of dollars in investment.

The Ottawa-Carleton Research Institute (OCRI) has helped position the capital as Canada's high-technology centre of excellence.

Opposite page **Entrepreneurs have discovered Ottawa's healthy business climate. The capital is home to many of the world's most innovative high-tech companies. Photo by Ari Tapiero.**

Our life sciences sector is experiencing tremendous growth, and the capital is becoming an internationally known centre for life sciences and biotechnology. Photo by Ari Tapiero.

entrepreneurial spirit. With over 200 members, the Women's Business Network is an active voice in the capital.

Government Resources in Our Backyard

Without question, Canada's capital is the logical choice for quick access to the various government departments which can help you do business both in and out of the country. It's where the decision-makers are; it's also where the information and resources our government offers are most readily at hand.

Commercial enterprises will find information and assistance from Industry Canada, the Department of Foreign Affairs and International Trade, the Export Development Corporation, the Canadian International Development Agency, the Conference Board of Canada and the Canadian Commercial Corporation, all headquartered in Ottawa.

The capital is also the base for the Canadian General Standards Board and the Standards

Council of Canada. Statistics Canada, which compiles a broad range of demographic and population data relevant to business, is an invaluable bank of information. And, of course, the National Research Council, the Department of National Defence, Health Canada and Agriculture Canada are important government resources for our high-tech sector.

Import and export procedures are crucial to the transaction of global business. Ports Canada, Transport Canada, Revenue Canada Customs and Excise and the NAFTA Secretariat here in Ottawa work with private enterprise to increase our national and cross-border trade.

There are other benefits in being close to Parliament Hill. The federal government is also one of the world's largest procurers of products and services. And with over 100 foreign consulates and embassies, Ottawa also provides additional opportunities to forge international business bonds.

Opposite page **The Plaza of Honour is located at the World Exchange Plaza. Each year, the Ottawa-Carleton Board of Trade pays tribute to successful capital entrepreneurs here. Photo by Ari Tapiero.**

Taking Care of Business–Expertise in Business Solutions

It's also important to have qualified professionals available to help you deal with your markets both in and out of the capital, and we have some of the best in the world. From market research and advertising agencies to customs brokers, patent and trademark agents and government relations specialists, you'll find the resources you need to help your business grow. Solutions to operating issues are easily found with our many office and technical support service companies, personnel agencies and accounting firms. In Ottawa, you're sure to find an expert to answer any and all of your questions, and a company to provide the assistance you need. We're in the business of doing business! ■

Businesses require expert advice, and Ottawa's experienced professionals stand ready to offer guidance and assistance. Courtesy Finlayson & Singlehurst. Photo by Jacqueline Turpin.

The Ottawa-Carleton Board of Trade is a key supporter of entrepreneurship and is an important networking organization for local businesses. Above, the area's success stories are applauded during the annual Business Achievement Awards. Photo by Eric Bawden.

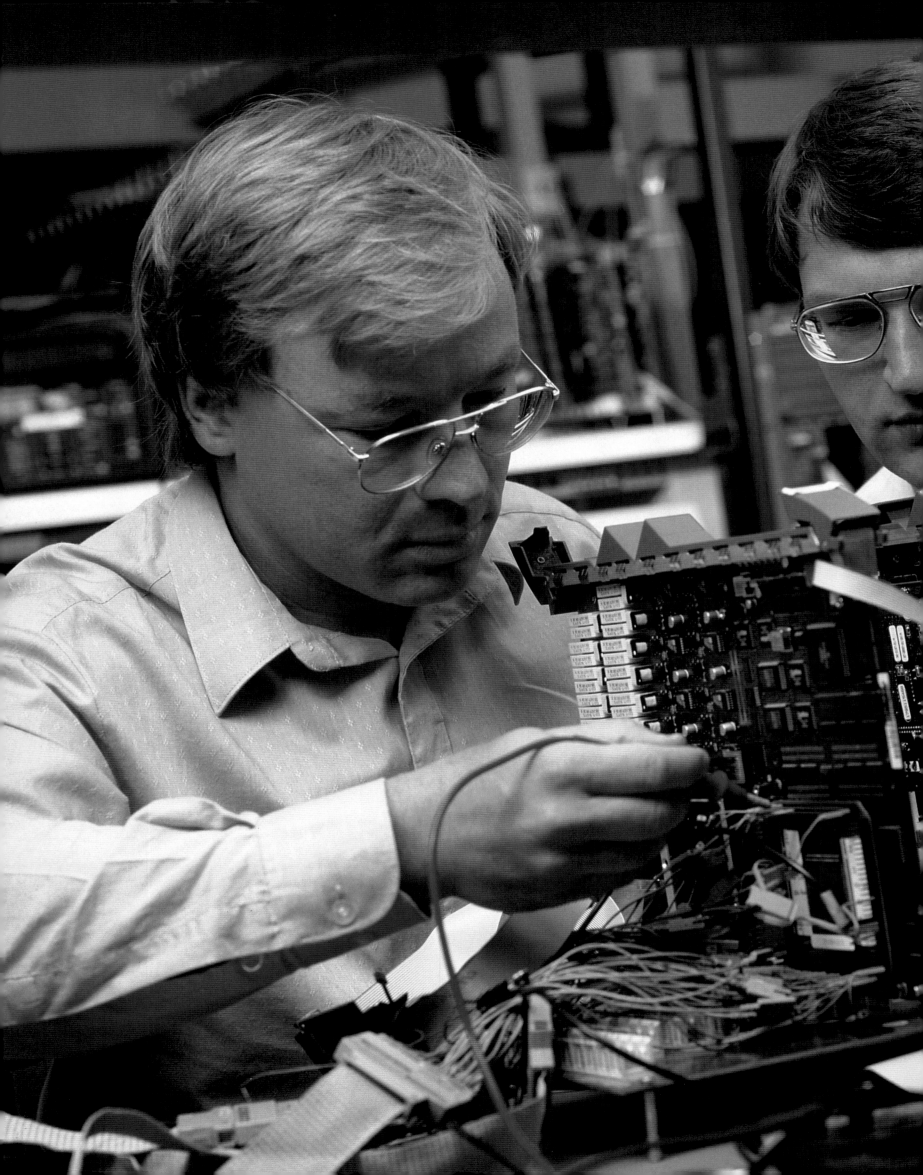

CHAPTER NINE

Capital Innovators—
The Leading Edge
in Technology

*T*he Ottawa region is known as "Silicon Valley

North" for good reason. Once an economy

predominantly driven by its government and public

sector base, Ottawa has evolved to become one of

North America's major centres for technological

innovation and manufacturing.

*H*igh technology in the public and private sectors now directly employs over 40,000 people in the capital, with an estimated 95,000 spin-off jobs, and generates more than $10 billion in revenues annually. Telecommunications, systems integration, software development, computer hardware and microchip design and manufacturing, satellite, aerospace and defence technology are thriving here, and many of our local companies are world leaders in their fields. The capital is also heading towards the forefront in the areas of life sciences and biotechnology, with major industries in radioisotopes, environmental technology and medical devices and research.

We boast the highest concentration of research and development in Canada. The government's National Research Council and other specialized research departments in Ottawa are staffed by over 10,000 scientists and professionals, and our private sector industries pump billions of dollars into research and development each year. The Canadian Space Agency's David Florida Laboratories are located here, with specialized testing facilities available to our high-tech community. The Canadian government's Department of National Defence has a significant presence here. And collaborative efforts such as the Ottawa-Carleton Research Institute and the Telecommunications Research Institute of Ontario, as well as the resources of other privately operated consortia, further open the doors to a wealth of information and expertise.

There are over 700 high-tech companies based in the Ottawa area today, the majority with certification of ISO 9000 or greater. Over 40 of these are publicly traded; you'll find them on the NYSE, the TSE, NASDAQ and other world exchanges. These corporations are here to reap the benefits of our highly educated, skilled, primarily non-union workforce, our cost-effective sites and facilities, our rich resources in terms of research and development, our proximity to government departments, our impressive technology transfer infrastructure and our cooperative, ongoing, aggressive marketing of the capital's high-tech sector as a whole. Quite simply, they're here because it's good business.

The High-Tech Sector—Spanning the Globe from a Capital Base

Here are some names you'll recognize: Nortel, Mitel Corporation, Newbridge Networks, Corel Corporation, Cognos Incorporated, SHL Systemhouse Ltd. (a division of MCI), JetForm Corporation, MOSAID Technologies Inc. They are just a few of the world leaders who have sprung from capital roots to make a global impact in the technologies market—and that's to name just a few on a list that keeps on growing.

Many other international firms also see the profit potential in maintaining an Ottawa base. American PC manufacturer Digital Equipment has a large manufacturing plant here. You'll find branch offices of Microsoft Canada Inc., Object Technology International (a subsidiary of IBM), Hewlett-Packard, Honeywell Limited, Sun Microsystems, Texas Instruments, Hitachi, Xerox, Lockheed Martin, AG Siemens and numerous others—all recognizing Ottawa's reputation as a global high-tech centre.

Here are a few examples of the high-tech companies that have chosen the capital as a business base. We can't possibly tell you about all 700 of them in one book, but we can tell you that one look at our high-tech base and you'll know Ottawa means business!

Telecommunications, Systems Integration and Fibre Optics

Nortel (Northern Telecom) is one of the world's largest telecommunications network developers. With an internationally respected research and development team, Nortel commits some $2.5 billion Canadian annually to research and development, and a large portion of that work is conducted right here in the capital. Over 8,000 professionals are based in Nortel's Ottawa research facilities, from engineers and software developers to scientists, lab technicians and management experts. In addition, Nortel employs nearly 2,500 people dedicated to manufacturing, marketing, operations and services. Many of today's Ottawa-based high-tech companies have evolved as a result of the presence of Nortel, widely regarded as the "grandfather" of Silicon Valley North.

Opposite page **Some of the world's most talented engineers, technicians and professionals are based right here in Ottawa's high-tech sector. Courtesy Computing Devices Canada.**

MITEL Corporation is another major player in the world's telecommunications field and has successfully branched out into the design and manufacture of semiconductors. From voice and network communications, public switching systems, CTI (computer telephony integration) systems and network enhancement and "gateway" products, MITEL was founded in the capital and was one of our first high-tech success stories. The company now employs 4,000 people worldwide with subsidiaries including MITEL Semiconductor and alliances with companies like Intel/Microsoft, Digital and many others. MITEL continues to make the capital its centre of operations.

Ottawa's Newbridge Networks is also recognized as an international leader in multimedia communications, with networking products and systems used by the world's 200 largest telecommunications providers. Newbridge's voice, data, image and video networks are also used by over 10,000 private and public firms, institutions and government organizations in virtually every continent. A 1997 study by *WorldLink* magazine and Deloitte & Touche Consulting Group placed Newbridge on the list of the world's 200 fastest growing companies. With 12 affiliated companies, Newbridge now employs over 4,000 people across the globe. Another 4,000 professionals will be hired by Newbridge here in Ottawa as part of the company's expansion plans, effectively doubling its workforce. The majority of its manufacturing takes place here in Ottawa, where the company was founded and where its world headquarters are based.

The pioneering force of SHL Systemhouse Inc. (an MCI company) began in 1974, when the communications company was established here in the capital. Now one of the world's leading system integrators, the company has over 90 offices worldwide and in 1995 became a wholly owned subsidiary of MCI Communications Corporation. SHL Systemhouse maintains its Canadian headquarters here in Ottawa with 1,200 employees.

The presence of major telecommunications companies here has had a spin-off effect. For example, JDS Fitel Inc., a world leader in fibre optics, took root in the capital in the early 1980s and is now the world's leading supplier of optical connector polishing equipment. The company also designs and manufactures optical switches, multiplexers, meters and test equipment and employs over 600 people.

Plaintree Systems, a manufacturer and developer of switching products for Ethernet and FDDI networks, maintains a strong capital presence and has developed an international reputation and client base. Founded in 1988, the company's research, development and manufacturing facilities are based here with over 160 employees, with its U.S. headquarters in Massachusetts.

Other telecommunications and systems integration firms with a capital presence include EDS Canada, iMPath Networks, CMI Technologies Inc., ISH (an IBM Company), Consultronics Limited and Centrepoint Technologies, along with many more.

Software Developers and Internet Innovators

Ottawa's Corel Corporation has become the world's second largest software company, competing directly with Microsoft in the "office suites" market. In just 10 years, this fast-growing, innovative corporation has vaulted up the ladder to international fame. Initial success came with its well-known "CorelDraw" graphics software, which continues to be a world leader, and Corel has gone on to diversify into other software applications with almost unprecedented success. With the acquisition of "WordPerfect" in 1996 and continued development of JAVA-based programs, CD-ROMs and interactive multimedia, its future looks bright indeed. Corel Corporation also made the list of the world's 200 fastest growing companies. Over 800 people work from Corel's Ottawa headquarters, with another 400 based in Utah.

Also making tremendous strides in the software market is Canada's second largest software company, Cognos Incorporated. Based in Ottawa for the past 25 years, Cognos has grown to become a major force in software development tools and end-user applications for business, with clients in nearly 60 countries and over 1,100 employees.

Fulcrum Technologies Inc. was founded in Ottawa in 1983 and now employs over 300 people to produce, market, license and support its indexing and retrieval software products. With 18 offices worldwide, Fulcrum counts companies like Microsoft and CompuServe among its clients.

Yet another Ottawa success story is Simware. Developing and supporting its Web, remote and LAN software has led to the creation of 140 jobs at its Ottawa headquarters and offices in Europe. Established in 1982, Simware's clients include

Opposite page **Newbridge Networks has an international presence and capital roots. The company is a recognized world leader in telecommunications. Courtesy Newbridge Networks.**

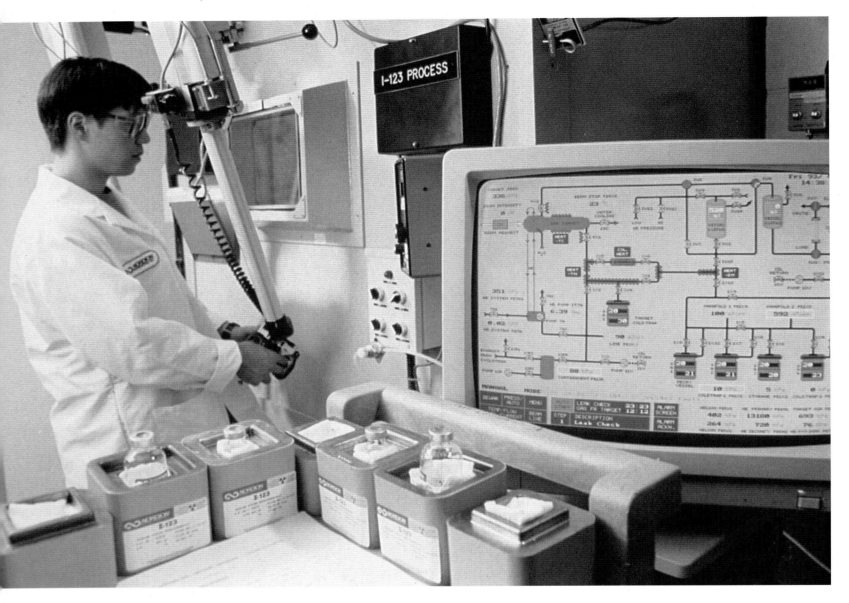

MDS Nordion blazed the trail for Ottawa's life sciences sector. The company was established here in 1946 and specializes in radioisotopes. Courtesy MDS Nordion.

the U.S. Departments of Justice and Commerce, Citibank and TNT.

JetForm Corporation was among the world's first companies to recognize the trend towards the "paperless office," and quickly became a leader in electronic "intelligent" forms technology. The result is a doubling in the number of employees to over 350 and the acquisition of Symantec's Delrina electronic forms division in 1996.

Software Kinetics, incorporated in 1981, is another classic example of a capital business start. Privately held and controlled by its 200 employees, the company retains its Ottawa roots with headquarters in Silicon Valley North and has operations in Nova Scotia as well. This software engineering and systems integration firm specializes in applications for communications, defence and aerospace.

*i*STAR internet inc. is among the premier Internet and Intranet service providers based in the capital, with nearly 250 employees. Also

making breakthroughs in the World Wide Web is Ottawa's Caravelle Inc., with its "WATCHER" software and other Internet monitoring tools.

There are numerous other software development companies in the high-tech capital, like Object Technology International (a subsidiary of IBM), Microstar Software Ltd., Quantum Information Resources Limited, Nuvo Networks, Milkyway Networks and a host of others.

Hardware, Computing Devices and Operating Systems

Another cornerstone of Silicon Valley North is Digital Equipment of Canada, a subsidiary of U.S.-based Digital Equipment Corporation. With a large manufacturing plant producing Intel-based PCs and high-speed Alpha servers and a large customer support centre, DEC's presence in the area has had a significant impact on the development of our high-tech sector. Since the manufacturing facility opened its doors in the region in 1972, it has expanded five times and today employs 1,400 workers.

The design and manufacture of memory chips and chip testing systems is the domain of Ottawa's MOSAID Technologies Incorporated. Established in 1975, the company's semiconductor division and systems division supply clients in the U.S., Japan, Korea, Taiwan and Europe and employ over 150 people. MOSAID maintains its headquarters in Silicon Valley North with additional facilities in Santa Clara, California, and Tokyo, Japan.

The innovative uses of laser technology have translated into success for Ottawa-based Lumonics Inc. From applications in the aerospace industry to automobiles and consumer products, Lumonics' laser-based manufacturing systems are providing solutions for cutting, laser welding, drilling and coding. Founded in 1971, Lumonics now has facilities around the world with over 875 employees,

some 275 of whom are based in the company's capital headquarters.

QNX Software Systems is a world leader in real-time multi-tasking operating systems for personal computers. Their technology allows standard PC hardware to handle the demands of complex and diverse industries ranging from factories, hospitals and laboratories to nuclear reactors and oil fields. Founded here in the capital in 1980, QNX counts among its clients over 100 companies on the *Fortune* 500 list.

Northern Micro Inc. has found success in manufacturing "clone" computers for a growing number of government and private sector clients. Among the capital's many other players in the hardware market are Chipworks, AIT Corporation, Semiconductor Insights, Optotek Ltd, MPC Circuits Inc. and Hardware Canada Computing.

Telecommunications giant Nortel continues to thrive in the capital. Poised for significant growth to accommodate the company's expansion, the Carling site is Nortel's largest research and product development location, encompassing more than 1.3 million square feet. Photo by Aker/Zvonkovic Photography LLP.

Satellite, Aerospace and Defence Technologies

Since its inception in 1948, Computing Devices Canada Inc. has been at the forefront of defence electronics and communications, including land, sea and air surveillance systems, voice and data communications, electronics for vehicles and systems integration. With 1,200 employees nation-wide (over 600 here in the capital), CDC remains on the cutting edge of technology and is now branching out into more commercial ventures, including electronic voting and payroll systems.

Spar Applied Systems employs over 2,600 workers in its international operations, with 300 of those specialists located here in the Ottawa area. Robotics, aviation and defence, space and ground communications and supporting software are the company's focus, including flight safety systems and naval communications systems used around the world.

CAL Corporation is another Ottawa-based pioneer in technology. Founded in 1974, this electromagnetic sciences company specializes in mobile satellite communications equipment, space scientific instruments and spacecraft power systems, as well as antennas, safety and surveillance equipment. Aircraft communications via satellite and aeronautical phone terminals are fast-growing components of CAL's services, and the company's 200 employees continue to be based in the capital.

Orbiting around the earth are the Anik satellites of Telesat Canada, based here in the capital with nearly 450 employees. Along with broadcasting over 55 television signals and moving into the fields of digital video compression and direct-to-home services, Telesat also serves private business by transmitting voice, data and image information. Its clients include many of Canada's major phone companies and broadcasting networks.

Calian Technology Ltd., with products and systems for satellite communications, employs nearly 500 people in Silicon Valley North. The company's divisions include SED Systems Inc., which specializes in systems engineering for satellite, space and defence, satellite testing and control and electronic system manufacturing. Calian Communications Systems Ltd. designs and manufactures terminal products, including a new pager which uses satellite transmissions. Its technical services sector provides professionals to government and industry.

Military and aerospace systems integrators make use of the technology of DY 4 Systems Inc., established in 1979 in Silicon Valley North. The company's large design and manufacturing plant is staffed by over 200 employees and provides board-level products and software, as well as support systems to clients in some 16 countries. DY 4's electronics are used in the B2 stealth bomber, F14 fighter jets and military tanks, as well as other defence and aerospace applications which require products to withstand unusually harsh conditions.

Thomson-CSF Systems Canada Inc., Lockheed-Martin, Siemens AG, Canadian Marconi and many other internationally known companies have established facilities in Ottawa because of our strong aerospace and defence sector.

Life Sciences and Biotechnology–On the Brink of the Next Millennium

The amazing strides in life sciences and biotechnology are changing the way we live, and the capital is poised to become one of North

Hundreds of local companies, such as Northern Micro, have evolved from small businesses to big successes. Courtesy Northern Micro.

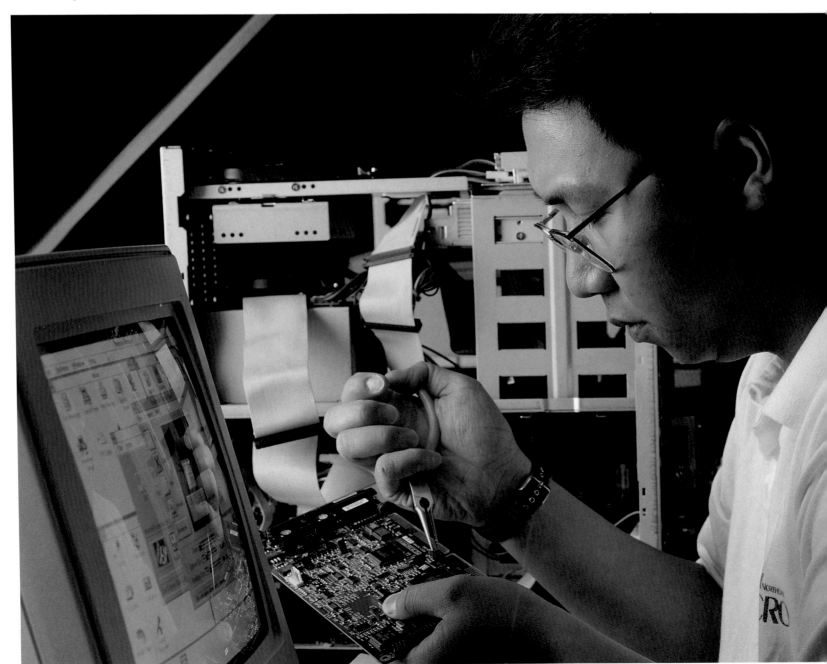

America's leading centres for these exciting new ventures. With the establishment of our Life Sciences Park and the rapidly growing concentration of biotech and life sciences companies here, as well as our internationally respected medical community and our university research programs, the capital is becoming a well-connected network. Products, technology and applications can be developed in concert with the professionals who will use them.

Leading the way towards the capital's life sciences and biotechnology boom has been Ottawa's MDS Nordion, an international corporation specializing in radioisotopes. Since it was established in 1946, the company has grown to employ over 600 people and become a world-respected provider of the products and technologies used in nuclear medicine and the sterilization of medical equipment. MDS Nordion also specializes in products that help companies eliminate harmful bacteria in food and in other types of consumer and pharmaceutical products.

Theratronics International is a major manufacturer and developer of radiation therapy systems used around the world for the treatment of cancer. Its main product lines are radiation therapy units and computer products which use specialized software to optimize cancer treatment planning. Based in the capital since 1965, Theratronics employs 250 specialists.

i-STAT Corporation produces blood analysis devices which are used in over 650 hospitals in the U.S., as well as in Japan, Mexico and South America. A recent alliance with Hewlett-Packard will see the company's products also distributed in Europe, Russia, Africa and the Middle East. Their facilities in the capital focus on research and manufacturing of sensors and employ 250 people.

A classic example of the successful network we've developed here in the capital is the new World Heart Corporation, which is striving to produce the world's first fully implantable permanent artificial heart. Using technology developed by the University of Ottawa Heart Institute, World Heart Corporation also has connections to the capital's high-tech sector through its major backers. SHL Systemhouse founder Rod Bryden (who operates SC Stormont Corporation and is the chairman of the Ottawa Senators and the Corel Centre) is the CEO of WorldHeart, and Dr. Michael Cowpland (founder and chairman of software giant Corel

Corporation) is also a major partner in the venture. WorldHeart hopes to begin clinical trials as early as 1999.

U.S. biotech giant Genzyme Corporation recently announced it will locate its Canadian headquarters here in the capital. And the breakthroughs now being made by Ottawa-based companies like Iogen Corporation, Fisher Scientific, Atlas Medical Resources Corporation and some 80 others will have a global impact on health and environmental concerns.

High-Tech Boomtown

Our flourishing high-tech sector brings to mind the gold rush of the 1800s, where thousands flocked to California and the north to stake their claims and make their fortunes. Today, in the world of high technology, it's happening right here. For along with the companies we've mentioned, there are literally hundreds of others here who are poised to take a place on the world's high-tech stage.

With starting salaries for Canadian engineers an estimated 25 per cent lower than their American counterparts and the superb education and training offered by our colleges and universities, which translates into a large pool of fresh graduate talent each year, Ottawa *is* Silicon Valley North. We're committed to continue that focus on, and into, the future. ■

Opposite page **MITEL was founded in the capital and was one of Ottawa's first high-tech success stories. Courtesy MITEL Corporation.**

Quatrosense Environmental Limited (QEL) designs, manufactures and services instrumentation focused primarily on the monitoring and control of emissions, environmental pollutants and industrial contaminants. Photo by Ari Tapiero.

Ottawa's Corel Corporation has grown to become the world's second largest software company. Photo by Ari Tapiero.

CHAPTER TEN

Capital Growth– Thriving on Enterprise & Change

*A*s Ottawa continues to evolve and expand

in terms of business, education and population,

we are well prepared for new development and

improved infrastructure to support our remark-

able growth. We're also proud of our track record

to date. Our region has a Triple-A financial rating;

there are no municipal income taxes; and many

of our municipalities are debt-free!

*W*ith improved transportation links, a solid bank of available sites for new business development and a steadily growing economy and population base, the capital is looking forward to a bright future.

Population and Economic Indicators

Economic health can often be assessed by the rate of population growth. Unlike many major cities, Ottawa is experiencing a sharp growth trend that is projected to continue over the next decade. There are over 1 million people in the capital region today. Over the past 10 years, our population has grown by nearly 18,000 people annually; many of them have arrived from other cities to take advantage of our thriving business climate. And we expect an additional 17 per cent increase in population during the next decade— that's nearly twice the standard growth rate for economically healthy communities.

And while economic trends across North America fluctuate from year to year, Ottawa has consistently remained an affluent community, with a high average annual income rate and an above-average rate of retail spending. In 1996, the average annual income in the region was approximately $24,000–that's among the top five in the country. Consumers here spend an average of $9,000 annually (per capita), with tourist retail dollars amounting to some $250 million of our total retail trade of $9 billion a year. That has translated into a wellspring of new business; over 1.3 million square feet of retail space were added to our area in 1996 alone!

Business Development Sites–Unlimited Resources and Expertise

Location, location, location–it's the credo of real estate, and Ottawa is among the most prestigious "addresses" in Canada. And as far as location within our region goes, there is a vast range of choice. With over 47 million square feet of existing office and industrial space in the capital, we boast the third-largest inventory of office space in the country. Over 27 million square feet of that is privately owned. Class "A" space can be found in the downtown district from $14 to $27 Canadian per square foot; taxes and operating costs start at about $11, and even more competitive rates can be found in other areas of the capital.

Industry has not only room, but also incentive,

to grow here. With over 40 established business parks and industrial areas, companies will find a niche for operations that make it convenient to network and conduct transactions with their clients, vendors and associates. In 1996, our average industrial net rental rate was just $4.75 Canadian per square foot.

The experience and expertise of the capital's development and construction industry is another motivating factor. With a wealth of skilled labour, construction costs here are an estimated 10 per cent lower than average compared to similar sites in the U.S. And Ottawa is home to some of the country's best-known and most highly regarded development corporations and commercial real estate companies, including Minto Developments, Glenview Corporation, Arnon Corporation, JJ Barnicke Ltd., Royal LePage and the Regional Group of Companies, among others.

A revitalization plan for our downtown core is underway, as innovative developers restore and renovate historical sites, office buildings and other underused properties to create new residential units and retail space.

The Ottawa market boasts stable housing prices, award-winning residential developments and room for new community growth. We enjoyed a 50 per cent increase in new housing starts in 1996, and the resale market remains strong and competitive with a wide range of prices and locations.

User-Friendly Utilities

Access to reliable and cost-effective utilities, capable of handling the demands of business and industry, is of paramount importance to commercial enterprise. Ottawa offers these resources in abundance.

Our current peak demand for water is at 72 per cent of our capabilities; it is also available at a competitive rate. Waste water treatment facilities here operate at rigid standards, and our treatment plants are state-of-the-art. The Robert O. Pickard treatment facility is able to process some 360 million gallons per day, and in 1996, was operating at 59 per cent capacity. With room to grow and continually upgraded equipment and processes, water and waste water treatment are available for new industrial ventures. The capital has also been a pioneer in terms of recycling and has provided protected sites for toxic waste materials.

Opposite page **Ottawa's many golf courses are an attraction in themselves and one reason for growth of the area's affluent sector. Courtesy Canadian Golf and Country Club.**

Ottawa has room to grow, and our healthy, diversified economy is paving the way towards an even brighter future. Photo by Ari Tapiero.

Electricity is another rich resource; Ontario Hydro is one of the world's largest electrical utilities and works with new clients to provide specialized requirements and competitive rates. With no forecast rate increases until the year 2000, electricity in the capital is stable and capable of supporting new major industrial ventures.

Ottawa also boasts the lowest gas distribution rates in the country. Consumers Gas can modify rates and supply to the specific needs of individual companies.

Communications in the capital are based on a solid foundation and are growing as technology changes. Bell Canada is the service provider for telecommunications in the capital, with a history of reliable service stretching back to its namesake. The cellular arm of Ottawa's telecommunications is supplied by Bell Mobility and Cantel Communications, among other providers.

Improved Highway Accessibility

One of the significant improvements now underway is a key extension of our main highway to link with one of the province's critical transportation routes. Highway 17, also known as the TransCanada Highway, runs directly through Ottawa-Carleton. As it extends into the capital, it becomes Highway 417, an eight-lane divided expressway which we refer to locally as the "Queensway." It's a busy route for both transport and commuter traffic, stretching from Montreal to the western provinces.

To the south, one of Canada's vital transportation links is Highway 401, the main route to Toronto and other major cities in southern Ontario with links to the U.S. border. A multi-year project by the Province of Ontario will create a connection between the TransCanada and Highway 401 from Ottawa. This strategic roadway will be known as Highway 416. Portions of the extension have already been finished, with a target date of the year 2000 for the completion of the convergence of the two thoroughfares.

While our current links to the 401, Highway 16 and Highway 7, continue to connect us to major centres in Canada and to the border, the new Highway 416 extension will mean quicker, streamlined accessibility both to and from the capital for import, export and commuter traffic.

On the Drawing Board

There are several projects "in the works" which we hope to see to fruition within the next few years. These include proposed plans for a major new hotel and convention facility in the downtown area, a hotel and office complex adjacent to the Corel Centre, and further expansion of our international airport.

Our capital growth is not an urban sprawl, nor is it an unchecked explosion of new population and industry. Rather, it is a carefully nourished, constantly monitored phase in our history that makes us one of the most envied regions in North America. We invite you to be a part of our "capital gains"! ■

A new four-lane highway to the south will create an express link to one of Canada's key transportation routes, Highway 401. Parts of the new Highway 416 are already open. Photo by Ari Tapiero.

**Ottawa International Airport
handles the flight needs of
millions of travellers each year.
Courtesy Air Canada. Photo
by Robert Zinck.**

**New U.S. customs pre-clearance
facilities are already in place
as part of the airport's major
expansion. Photo by Ari Tapiero.**

Photo by Ari Tapiero

A Contemporary Portrait
PART TWO 2

CHAPTER ELEVEN

Networks

Photo by Ari Tapiero

Between 1983 and 1987, a $52.8-million renovation of the terminal was completed, and today, Ottawa International is one of the most modern airports in Canada.

The Airport Authority is developing the services and facilities of the airport, exploring new ways of doing business and forging new partnerships.

There are two separate terminals that are major fixed-based operators to cater to the requirements of private and chartered aircraft.

in traffic upon the signing of the Open Skies Agreement with the U.S. in February 1995. Several airlines established new links into major American cities, including Detroit, Chicago and Washington, D.C., and these new flights virtually tripled the airport's "lift capacity" from 1,000 to 3,000 seats per day.

Ottawa International's Facilities and Services "In Flight"

Like the community it serves, the airport's business is vibrant. The National Capital Region, besides hosting the country's national Parliament, is home to dynamic international companies like Nortel, Corel, and Newbridge, and boasts some of the most remarkable tourist events in the world. These advantages of the region, plus the most recent passenger traffic studies indicating solid, long-term passenger increases of two to three per cent annually, signal new growth and an expanded role in the development of the region for Ottawa International.

Many recognize the airport as an economic lever of the community; yet, in its own right, it makes a significant contribution to the region's economy. In 1996, Ottawa International served 2.5 million passengers and handled 162,000 aircraft movements. The airport accounts for approximately 4,700 direct and indirect jobs that produce an $85-million total wage bill per year. In fact, the airport generates $240 million of economic output annually within the region. With this economic activity, Ottawa International is a self-sufficient entity and a net generator of wealth for the National Capital Region.

Currently, Air Canada, Canadian Airlines, American Airlines and a number of smaller carriers like Greyhound Airlines, First Air, USAir and Bearskin Airlines fly passengers and goods across Canada and into several major U.S. cities–Chicago, Detroit, Pittsburgh, Washington, D.C., Newark, Philadelphia and Boston. The new preclearance facility, coupled with the region's tremendous growth potential, suggests ever-increasing opportunities for airlines and the travelling public.

Though Ottawa International is one of the most modern airports in Canada, the Airport Authority's Board of Directors and management is intent on advancing the facility and improving its services. Airport President and CEO Paul Benoit states the objectives as threefold: to improve customer service and satisfaction; make more efficient use of the facility and develop first-class services; and forge new partnerships with local business and community groups.

Improving customer service and satisfaction will mean travellers can expect to enjoy expanded and upgraded services. For instance, they can expect a wider choice of retail and duty-free shopping, and a better selection of restaurants and first-class lounges. Most importantly, with the facility now privately managed, travellers can come to expect a more customer-oriented approach to services.

The Airport Authority's second objective of developing the services and facilities of the airport points to new ways of doing business. Today, the airport's 5,000-acre site is used by carriers serving Canada, the U.S. and Europe. Airport traffic is served by the two main runways running north-south and east-west on the property. A review of the current usage and expansion options of the airport property to accommodate further increases in traffic are the core issues to be studied and resolved for Ottawa International's multi-year master plan.

The airport's many tenants will continue to play an integral role in the development of the facilties and services. There are two separate terminals, the Esso-Avitat and Shell Aerocentre, that are major fixed-based operators catering to the requirements of private and chartered aircraft. In addition to the passenger transit and freight facilities at the main terminal building, Ottawa

International is base to the Ottawa Flying Club (the longest serving tenant for nearly 70 years); Transport Canada's fleet of training aircraft; the RCMP's and Canadian Forces' aircraft; and Laurentian Air Services Ltd., a commercial airline that serves the eastern Arctic. Transport Canada's Flight Services Directorate is based at the field, along with a training facility for air traffic controllers. The airport also has a number of research facilities operated by the National Research Council (NRC) of Canada.

The third important objective for the Airport Authority is the fostering of new working relationships with community organizations. The priority for the latter part of 1997 is initiating public consultations and a multi-year master plan process. These consultations, and the creation of the Airport Authority's master plan, will provide the blueprint for the airport's growth. With public input through the process, the master plan will ensure that the airport effectively develops its facilities and services into the new century, and meets the needs of the stakeholders it serves and affects.

A Community-Based, International Airport

As the National Capital Region has blossomed into an exciting tourist destination and the driving force of Canada's high-technology industry, Ottawa International continues to evolve to meet the new demands and exceed the expectations of the capital's travelling public. It is paradoxical that, as a growing region forces its airport to expand, a growing airport propels its region to the world.

Ottawa International has come of age as a not-for-loss, business-focused, community-based airport. It is a significant economic player that is actively fostering new business partnerships to contribute to the growth of the region and to promote the region as a place to visit and do business. With its unique mix of commercial, government, military and general aviation traffic, and with its range of facilities and services like the NRC and freight research activities, Ottawa International offers innovative and unparalleled opportunities to the residents of the National Capital Region and to those who visit it. ■

The bulk of Ottawa International's traffic is served by the two main runways running north-south and east-west on the airport's 5,000-acre site. A review of the current usage and expansion options of the airport property are the core issues to be studied and resolved for Ottawa International's multi-year master plan.

The Ottawa Sun

Bright and on the rise—that's the *Ottawa Sun*, the National Captal Region's newest and fastest-growing English daily newspaper.

A mass-circulation tabloid, the *Sun* is known for its brash editorial style, with an emphasis on local news, sports and lively opinion columns.

Hometown girl Alanis Morissette has made her fellow Ottawans proud with her record-breaking CD, *Ironic*. Photo by Denis Cyr.

To get to know the *Sun's* personality, look no further than its mission statement: "We publish outspoken and fair newspapers and information for our readers, advertisers, staffers and communities. In doing so, we strive to be open, innovative, caring, competitive, profitable and fun."

And that's not all that's unusual about the *Sun*.

Like the *Sun*, the NHL's Ottawa Senators have risen steadily since their inception in 1990. Photo by Derek Ruttan.

Unique among Canadian newspapers, the *Ottawa Sun* is employee-owned and run. *Sun* management and staff bought the newspaper from Rogers Communications Inc. in the fall of 1996— a time when local papers across the industry were being bought up by big international publishing conglomerates.

Reflecting the company's success, the *Ottawa Sun's* staff has multiplied nearly 10 times since the newspaper was founded in 1988.

It all started when the local owners of the floundering *Ottawa Sunday Herald* approached the Toronto Sun Publishing Corporation to buy the paper.

The *Sun* took up the offer, doubled the staff of 26 and launched the *Ottawa Sunday Sun* in September 1988.

The community's response was so positive that two months later the newspaper expanded into larger premises and began publishing daily—on November 7, 1988.

By January 1990, the *Sun* had prospered enough to buy its own building and printing press. At this point, 35 skilled jobs were created to handle the newspaper's production, and the *Sun* absorbed local pressmen who had been laid off when the French-language paper closed its printing facility.

To keep up with technological change and the paper's expanding needs, the *Sun* acquired four more press units in 1995. As well, the company added state-of-the-art equipment for automatically inserting separate sections of the paper, making its printing plant one of the most advanced facilities in Eastern Ontario. The plant now has 70 full- and part-time employees and also does commercial printing for other major publications. *Ottawa Sun* staff now totals over 240, excluding wholesalers and carriers.

Since the *Sun's* rise, Ottawa-Carleton's economy has seen a major shift. From the 1960s through the 1980s, it had been dominated by the federal public service, the region's main employer. But government downsizing and dramatic growth in the high-tech and business sectors have changed the face of the capital.

The *Sun* has mirrored that change in its own entrepreneurial evolution and pro-business stance.

The *Sun* has won numerous awards for creative excellence in advertising and promotion, as well

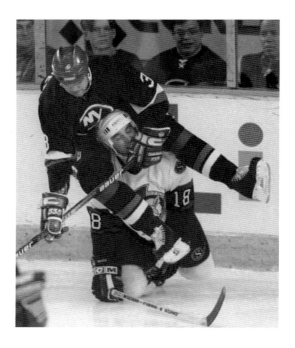

as for its extraordinary year-to-year increase in circulation. According to the Audit Bureau of Circulation, which tracks media penetration of the market, the *Ottawa Sun* was the fastest growing newspaper in Canada for the six months ending March 31, 1996.

The paper's share of the circulation and advertising market continues to expand, along with its coverage of news, sports and entertainment.

Over the years, the *Sun* has added special editorial features and sections reflecting readers' interest in sports, health and local and national politics, along with issues important to the local business community.

As well, the *Sun* has been a leader in exploring national issues–it broke the story on the military coverup in Somalia, among many others–and international issues, as seen in last fall's series on the plight of children around the world.

Stories like these have helped the *Sun* win several accolades for editorial quality and design. In the past four years, the *Sun* has won three National Newspaper Award nominations, Canada's top professional prizes for journalistic excellence.

And the awards don't end there.

Sun writers, editors, photographers and cartoonists have been recognized with many other awards. Notable among these are the Edward Dunlop Awards, which recognize achievement throughout the *Sun* newspaper chain. To date, the *Sun* has received 16 Dunlop citations for excellence in writing, photography and design. In 1995 alone, the *Sun* was also given two awards and an honorable mention by the Canadian Nurses Association for excellence in health reporting.

Reflecting the *Sun*'s corporate culture, staff members are also active in the community.

Several senior staff sit as directors on the boards of the Ottawa General Hospital, the University of Ottawa Heart Institute and the Children's Hospital of Eastern Ontario. The company also contributes more than $500,000 a year of promotional space to some 400 community charities, non-profit volunteer organizations and community events.

To help boost tourism, the region's largest industry, the *Sun* has sponsored Winterlude–the internationally recognized winter carnival–for several years and widely promoted Ottawa-Carleton's bid for EXPO 2005.

Sun journalists also do their part to share their professional expertise with journalism students

A water-skier struts his stuff on the Rideau River, a year-round playground for outdoor enthusiasts. Photo by Jeff Bassett.

at Algonquin College and Carleton University–through classroom teaching, mentoring and internship programs.

As well, to encourage academic excellence, the *Ottawa Sun* has established a $1,500 award to be given each year to an outstanding journalism student from either school. ■

Great photography becomes a great newspaper. *Sun* staffer Fred Sherwin's photo of a man catching fire has been nominated for a National Newspaper Award. Photo by Fred Sherwin.

iSTAR internet inc.

T he rapid advance of Internet technology has created a sea change in the way information is managed and handled, impacting the way we communicate, the way we educate and the way we link our home and work spaces—to each other, and to the world.

*i*STAR internet inc. believes that the pace of the future is even more breathtaking than that of the past. As Canada's leading commercially focused Internet solutions company, it is already riding the next wave of Internet technology with competitive innovations such as *i*NTRANET and *i*COMMERCE®.

Created in 1995 through the merger of NSTN Incorporated and i*internet Inc., *i*STAR's experience in the Internet solutions industry is unrivalled. Headquartered in Ottawa, the company has built a fully national data/voice/image network infrastructure which over 80 per cent of the population can access with a local call.

Through this network, *i*STAR offers the broadest range of commercial services available, including roaming, Intranets, electronic commerce, security, network integration, network operation centres and help desks. Eight advanced computer centres in Canada's largest cities provide customers with the industry's highest level of network management and round-the-clock technical support capabilities.

The strength of *i*STAR's people, the best and brightest in the business, drives these achieve-

ments. Nationally, the company has brought together commercially focused sales, professional support and technical support groups. In Ottawa, strong computer and telecommunications expertise merge in the management, engineering and marketing teams. Throughout the company, *i*STAR's people provide clients with a level of care, support and service that is second to none.

Such talent and enthusiasm have earned *i*STAR a unique position. Much more than an Internet access provider, the company provides organizations with solutions that truly harness the power of the Internet.

In many ways, the Internet today can be compared to the early days of the automobile, when, to keep the car on the road, a driver had to be a mechanic as well. *i*STAR places great importance on its technical support and help desk services as a result, ensuring that drivers always have access to mechanics, helping clients fully explore the technology's power.

Harnessing the Power of Change

Internet technology has brought with it fundamental and profound changes in communication and information management. While individual companies may already have new information structures up and running, the Internet provides a communication system to link those who, although outside the company, are an integral part of its distribution or sales system.

Take, for example, a doctor who sends a patient's prescription information to a pharmacy. The patient may be one of three types of potential customers: regular patients seeking wellness; those looking to resell the drugs; or those in danger of abusing the prescription, by combining it with other drugs, for instance. A network that links individual doctors and pharmacies, thereby showing a prescription history, could immediately recognize into which category a patient falls, preventing the second- or third-category patients from obtaining potentially harmful drugs.

*i*STAR's focus on such Internet applications places it—and its customers—on the cutting edge of the industry.

The company's development of *i*NTRANET, for example, tailors the features of the Internet to a client's specific needs. An Intranet functions as a company's private Internet, accessing and yet securely isolated from the public Internet, with security often supplemented through encryption and electronic authorization.

*i*NTRANET's unique solution incorporates a LAN/WAN gateway to the Internet, coupled with an encrypted link, firewalls, network monitoring and consulting services–in a single turnkey package.

In another application, Forrester Research estimates that Canadian consumer spending via the Internet could reach $3.2 billion by 2001. Until recently, however, maintaining the security of information such as credit card numbers over the Internet limited its full application as a sales tool.

*i*STAR's *i*COMMERCE® solution now offers businesses the opportunity to reliably and securely process orders from Web site customers–via existing World Wide Web browser technology. *i*COMMERCE® features customer and merchant authentication; secure transaction and payment authorization and processing; and customer tracking tools to determine buying trends, in a user-friendly, cost-effective package.

Even without electronic commerce, maintaining a presence on the World Wide Web has become essential to many companies' communication and marketing plans. For those wanting a high-quality Web site without the expense and resources required to manage it themselves, *i*STAR offers Canada's premier Web hosting services.

*i*STARWEB offers corporations mid-range and high-end hosting services: clients access not only the best current and future Web site design tools, but also the expertise of *i*STAR's award-winning design teams.

The CTV Television Network/*i*STAR Web site, created for the March 1997 World Figure Skating Championships, gained immediate popularity, receiving 8 million hits in one week–telling testimony to the strength of *i*STAR's network and server infrastructure.

Of course, *i*STAR's reputation also stands on the quality Internet access products it offers, including dedicated and dial access services, and business solutions for such challenges as LAN/WAN integration, security, network design, server configuration, installation and management.

Riding the Next Wave

*i*STAR's national network and extensive knowledge are increasingly sought after, as the company shifts to professional services as a computer engineering firm offering a range of back office functions–including consulting services to

fax, telephone and cable companies as they prepare to enter the industry.

Further demonstrating *i*STAR's commitment to clients is its introduction of CyberPatrol, free blocking software that lets parents, caregivers and teachers block Internet sites containing offensive or inappropriate information. "Safety Net" is part of the company's national awareness campaign that includes Internet guidelines for child safety. The company was also instrumental in drafting the Canadian Association of Internet Providers' code of conduct.

As the tide of Internet technology change continues to rush in, *i*STAR's strategy as a deployer of software, identifying and purchasing the best new Internet applications and customizing them to meet the particular needs of its clients, will continue to reap rewards and ensure that *i*STAR internet inc. will remain at the forefront of the industry, translating its focus on service into its clients' worldwide success. ■

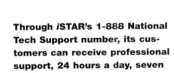

*i*STAR's unique coast-to-coast backbone is exclusively dedicated to Internet traffic. Local access is gained through over 40 points of presence (POPs) across the country, and multiple connections to both ANS and MCI networks in the U.S.

Through *i*STAR's 1-888 National Tech Support number, its customers can receive professional support, 24 hours a day, seven days a week.

Air Canada

Daily service from Ottawa to such business centres as Chicago, Washington, Newark and Boston means new destinations for Air Canada's customers, who can sit back, relax and enjoy the most convenient and comfortable transborder air service available.

Air Canada and its regional airlines provide air service for passengers and cargo to 125 destinations around the world. Together with its global alliance partners, the airline offers its customers over 500 destinations in more than 100 countries.

With the addition of 41 new aircraft through 1998, Air Canada boasts one of the youngest fleets of aircraft in the world. New aircraft add up to new services like Ottawa to Washington. And, Air Canada is the only airline offering daily direct international service from Ottawa to Europe.

It's a world of service that began 60 years ago. Canada's largest air carrier inaugurated its first flight September 1, 1937, as Trans-Canada Air Lines (TCA). The 50-minute flight aboard a Lockheed 10A carried two passengers and mail between Vancouver and Seattle. By 1964, TCA had grown to become Air Canada, Canada's national airline, with a growing international network.

The carrier's distinctive maple leaf is recognized around the world as the company operates an average of more than 500 scheduled flights every day, serving more than 11 million passengers each year.

easier and faster between the world's two largest trade partners. Daily service from Ottawa to such business centres as Chicago, Washington, Newark and Boston means new destinations for Air Canada's customers, who can sit back, relax and enjoy the most convenient and comfortable transborder air service available. Closer to home, Air Canada's wholly owned regional airlines–AirBC, Air Ontario, Air Alliance, Air Nova and NWT Air–serve 46 Canadian and 12 American cities using a combined fleet of 82 aircraft. The regional airlines carry more than 3.7 million passengers a year on over 600 flights a day, making them the fifth largest regional airline group in North America and the sixth largest in the world.

This success at home and abroad reveals the degree of customer loyalty that Air Canada has achieved through focusing on value-added customer service, technical excellence and passenger safety.

Air Canada's Rapidair service in the key business triangle between Ottawa, Montreal and Toronto offers a sterling example of the company's approach: the best schedules, the most flights and the newest planes, every business day. With the first flight out and the last flight home, dedicated check-in and departure gates, the most legroom and on-board phone, fax and e-mail service, Rapidair makes business travel a breeze.

For leisure travellers, Air Canada Vacations offer vacation packages to more than 60 destinations. Some 150,000 passengers a year take advantage of these packages, which feature everything from air travel, accommodations and car rentals to cruises and ski vacations.

The cargo division, meanwhile, provides direct

Local member of Parliament, Mrs. Marlene Catterall, joins Hollis Harris, in a ribbon-cutting ceremony commemorating the Ottawa-Washington inaugural flight.

Focused on Flight

An Air Canada snapshot reveals scheduled passenger jet service to cities in Canada, the United States, Europe, the Caribbean, the Middle East and Asia. Charter services fly to six international destinations, while alliances with other major international air carriers, including United, Lufthansa, SAS, All Nippon Airways, Korean Air and Swissair, further extend the company's global reach.

The 1995 Canada - U.S. Open Skies agreement provides Air Canada with the opportunity to make travel

air cargo service to Air Canada passenger destinations, and to most countries worldwide through interline agreements. Products include air freight, door-to-door service, and guaranteed, same-day, airport-to-airport service for high-priority shipments.

Centred on Service

Air Canada prides itself on catering to the needs of business travellers. Most North American flights offer Executive Class, which provides the comfort and personal attention needed for business people to arrive at their destinations refreshed, composed and at ease. It's a definite business asset, with priority check-in, baggage handling and boarding; a choice of meals on most flights; and on-board phones within hand's reach.

For international travellers, Executive First encompasses all the features of first class for the price of business class. Available on most transatlantic and all transpacific routes, it pampers passengers with more room to rest, and more room to work; lots of personal space, a 21-inch wide reclining electronic sleeper seat, and global access telephones. That's just the beginning. For relaxation, Executive First passengers enjoy award-winning entertainment from the video screen right at their seat.

Customers who want to work or relax before a flight find quiet, comfortable havens in Air Canada's Maple Leaf Lounges. Located at key airports around the world, they welcome Executive First passengers, Aeroplan Elite members, Maple Leaf Club members and Diners/enRoute Maple Leaf Club cardholders.

Air Canada also assists meeting planners. Whether it's a meeting for 10 or 10,000, the carrier flies delegates from more places in Canada than any other airline to hundreds of destinations around the world. Travel counsellors make meetings a fiscal success with advantages such as special North American convention rates, complimentary tickets and savings on air cargo rates and car rentals.

Earning customer loyalty means the world to Air Canada: more than 3 million Air Canada customers belong to the airline's frequent flyer program, Aeroplan, earning miles toward free travel through an extensive array of airline, hotel and transport partners and affinity cards.

Royal Canadian Mounted Police Sgt. Pierre Chartrand takes part in the celebration honouring the Ottawa-Washington inaugural flight.

It isn't just passengers who have come to rely on the company. Air Canada's leading position in the global air transportation market is recognized in the services it extends to the travel industry. Its Galileo system is the sole Canadian-owned-and-operated provider of computer reservation products and services for such travel companies as airlines, railways, cruise lines, hotels and tour operators.

The air carrier also shares its expertise in the maintenance and overhaul of aircraft, engines, components and various ground and test equipment. And, knowing Air Canada's track record for quality, other airlines have become customers for ground handling services and training services for mechanics, flight attendants and pilots.

Air Canada's Ottawa operations embody the company's philosophy of providing outstanding support and hassle-free travel to its passengers, cargo shippers and business clients. Across Canada, into the United States, and around the world—Air Canada works to make its customers feel right at home. ■

Air Canada's distinctive maple leaf is recognized around the world as the company operates an average of more than 500 scheduled flights every day, serving more than 11 million passengers each year.

Bell Canada

As Canada's oldest and largest telecommunications company, Bell Canada has been a household word in Ontario and Quebec for over 115 years. But there is a lot more to Bell Canada than telephones, especially in today's rapidly evolving telecommunications industry. A highly competitive company operating in an increasingly dynamic marketplace, Bell is a world leader in providing reliable and innovative voice, data and image communications.

With over 40,000 employees and more than 7 million customers in Ontario and Quebec, Bell Canada is also a key economic contributor in terms of employment, capital spending, R&D and product and service development. And through business alliances with companies in related industries—including the software, manufacturing, retail and multimedia sectors—Bell is consistently "pushing the envelope" in delivering advanced, low-cost telecom solutions to customers.

In basic terms, Bell Canada currently provides local, long-distance and, through its cellular affiliate Bell Mobility, wireless telephone services. But within these broad categories are a large number of specialized services designed to meet the specific needs of individual customers, whether residential long distance users, home-based businesses or large corporate accounts.

Among these services are 800/888 and 900 long distance services; basic and high-speed Internet access; video and audio teleconferencing; high-speed data transmission services; Wide Area Network (WAN) and Local Area Network (LAN) services; an array of enhanced SmartTouch™ features, including Call Answer and Call Display; and services for customers with special needs.

Supporting all of these products and services are complex technologies not readily apparent to the consumer. Bell's long distance network, for example, is fully served by digital switches, providing an advanced electronic backbone that supports the latest state-of-the-art products and services. Bell's local network is more than 90 per cent digital, and the company plans to be fully digitized by the end of 1997 (July 1998 in the Far North) as part of a major network modernization program.

Through corporate sponsorship and employee involvement, Bell Canada is committed to supporting the well-being of the communities it serves through numerous organizations and special programs. Since 1990, for example, Bell has contributed more than $4 million a year in sponsorships, touching almost every aspect of Canadian life. The Boys and Girls Clubs of Canada, the Kids Help Phone and the United Way are just a few of the initiatives Bell sponsors.

Bell Canada also supports a wide range of cultural institutions, including the Stratford Festival (since 1953) and the Governor General's Performing Arts Awards. On the professional sports front, Bell is a sponsor of the NHL's Ottawa Senators as well as the annual Bell Canadian Open golf tournament.

While Bell Canada's corporate headquarters are located in Montreal, the company maintains a large presence in Ottawa. Bell's Ottawa-based operations, for example, include numerous groups devoted to marketing as well as key regulatory and policy issues affecting Canada's telecommunications industry (hotbeds of activity in recent years given the rapid roll-out of competition).

As well, the company's operations in Ottawa work closely on the development of new products and services, tapping the resources of other Ottawa-based technology companies which, collectively, constitute what is commonly referred to in industry circles as Silicon Valley North. ■

Bell Canada's Internet Service, Sympatico

The Consumers Gas Company Ltd.

More than 1.4 million customers in Ontario rely on Consumers Gas to supply them with natural gas to heat their homes and businesses, fuel their vehicles and power their manufacturing processes.

Established in 1848, Consumers Gas is Canada's oldest and largest gas distribution company, offering a long history of stability, reliability and responsibility.

That rich heritage encourages commercial, residential and industrial customers to turn to Consumers Gas both for natural gas delivery and a wide range of innovative services. Through research and development of new technology, carefully planned pipeline extensions and expert advisory services, Consumers Gas offers its customers not just a commodity, but a resource.

The company's leading development efforts include contributions to the development of high-efficiency furnaces, natural gas fuel systems for commercial fleet vehicles, and cogenerational technology, which involves the simultaneous production of electricity and heat from one fuel source. The advantages of natural gas fuel this focus on development: clean-burning and cost-competitive, natural gas systems produce less pollution and run at lower costs.

In such rapidly growing Ottawa-Carleton communities as Orleans, Cumberland, Gloucester, Kanata and Nepean, approximately 90 per cent of new homes install natural gas. And natural gas plays a key energy efficiency role from Hershey Canada's Smiths Falls operation to the National Gallery Canada, from the Rideau Centre to the steam boilers and turbines of Parliament Hill's heating and cooling plant.

In addition, most of the region's high-technology firms use natural gas. Whether the firms produce computers, telecommunications components and systems, electronics for military and scientific use, or satellite systems, natural gas helps keep energy costs in line and contributes to a clean, dust-free environment for microchip production.

Ottawa-Carleton itself provides the key administrative and operational location for the Eastern Region of Consumers Gas. Here, more than 3,500 kilometres of mains deliver about 1.4 billion cubic metres of natural gas annually. Affiliate and subsidiary companies serve another 25,000 customers in western Quebec and northern New York State.

Although natural gas became available in 1958, manufactured gas was long used in Ottawa-Carleton: in 1856, the City of Ottawa had gas street lamps, while in 1867, gas provided lighting in the new Parliament Buildings.

In 1957, The Consumers' Gas Company Limited purchased two Ottawa-area utilities which continued to operate under their own names until 1987, when the company became known as Consumers Gas. Today, 280 dedicated employees provide a full range of services and expertise. In keeping with the community-oriented, regionally focused philosophy of Consumers Gas, these employees support many charitable and non-profit organizations. The Little Gas House at 1135 Carling Avenue, for example, provides accommodation for families of out-of-town patients undergoing treatment at Ottawa Civic Hospital.

The roots of Consumers Gas are set firmly in its heritage of responsible service to the businesses, residents and industries in its communities. The company's expertise, supply and service capability, meanwhile, will continue to serve those who seek a clean-burning, economical and versatile resource: natural gas is their fuel of choice. ■

Piping a new subdivision— 90 per cent of new homes use natural gas.

The Little Gas House is symbolic of Consumers Gas community involvement.

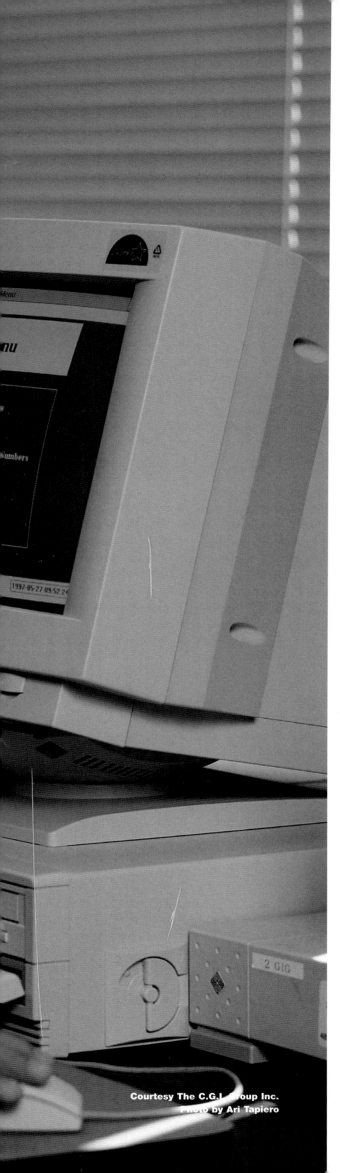

CHAPTER TWELVE

High Technology & Manufacturing

MOSAID Technologies Incorporated

The current phenomenal growth of multimedia, information technology and telecommunications relies not only on the increased speed and power of processors, but, just as importantly, on memory. As the industry leader in memory chip design and testing, MOSAID Technologies Incorporated helps almost every memory chip designer and manufacturer worldwide.

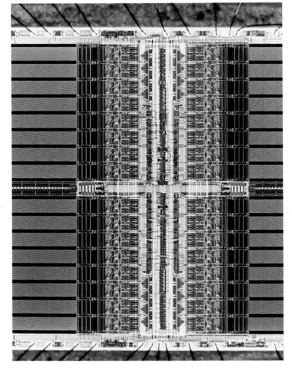

The MOSAID 16M SDRAM design in volume production

From computers, cellular phones and compact disc players to automobiles and fax machines, memory is everywhere.

MOSAID derives its name from AIDing MOS designers—MOS means Metal Oxide Semiconductor, the construction material for most memory chips. These semiconductor memory chips, or memory integrated circuits (ICs), play an ever-increasing role in our daily lives. In personal computers and their operating system software, in automobiles and video games, even in household "smart" appliances like kitchen stoves, ICs bring to life the concepts of smaller, better and faster.

When MOSAID Technologies Incorporated was founded in 1975, the worldwide memory chip industry was worth about $30 million a year, and silicon chips held 4,000 bits of memory storage capacity. Today's chips hold over 16 million bits, while annual sales have rocketed to more than $30 billion.

MOSAID is not only the world's leading independent memory chip design house, but also the leading supplier of memory engineering test systems. Its experience and expertise enable it to develop complex IC designs on budget and on schedule, while its independence gives it a broad perspective on the global memory business.

Because it is not tied to a proprietary technology, MOSAID is uniquely positioned to support technologies that will be the industry's future mainstay products. To achieve this, it relies on the synergy created by its two closely related operating divisions.

The Semiconductor Division designs advanced memory chips for chip manufacturers and has done so for every generation of memory since the company was founded. MOSAID licenses its designs, earning royalties once the chips go into production. Thanks to its innovative work, the company holds 36 patents, with over 90 patent applications pending worldwide.

The Systems Division designs, manufactures, sells and supports engineering test systems that companies use to evaluate memory chips that will go into production–a market segment MOSAID pioneered and continues to advance.

Making this synergy work are MOSAID's people. MOSAID fosters an entrepreneurial environment through a flat, not hierarchical, structure, enhancing a team approach. That people have a voice in the direction of their projects is reflected in the company's ability to attract and retain people with the skills and expertise necessary to achieve superior designs under tight deadlines, and to focus on the needs of customers.

Employee-oriented programs, and ongoing training such as MOSAID's in-house IC layout design course, allow employees to combine their goals with those of the company.

As a result, MOSAID leads the memory development field. Where memory once evolved steadily–every three years, a new generation packed more memory into basically the same structure–the form and types of memory architecture are now diversifying at astronomical rates.

On the cutting edge of memory design technology, MOSAID works with the SLDRAM consortium in developing a new, high-performance standard for communication between memory and computer processors.

The consortium–which also includes Fujitsu, Hitachi, Hyundai, IBM Micro Electronics, LG Semicon, Matsushita, Micron, Mitsubishi, NEC,

Nippon Steel, Oki, Samsung, Texas Instruments, Toshiba, Vanguard, Motorola, Siemens, Mosel Vitelic, Apple, Hewlett-Packard and IBM awarded MOSAID a key design engineering contract to examine the system feasibility, chip architecture and bus interface of this new technology.

The company also works with industry leaders at the Joint Electron Device Engineering Council (JEDEC), an international body that sets standards for electronic devices. Helping to establish parameters and specifications for future memory product generations directly benefits MOSAID's customers through the company's design work. JEDEC has recognized MOSAID as a centre of excellence for its ground-breaking work with tomorrow's mainstay product: Synchronous Dynamic Random Access Memory (SDRAM).

SDRAM's significance lies in speed. Where traditional, non-synchronous DRAM chips could reach data input/output rates ranging from 10 to 20 MHz, SDRAM can match rates up to 200 MHz. That speed impacts PC design, increasing system performance and reducing the cost of high-performance PCs and workstations.

MOSAID identified SDRAM's potential very early. As a result, the industry already relies upon MOSAID's designs, mirroring the company's success with DRAM: MOSAID has the world's most respected DRAM design team, and has designed every generation of DRAM since the industry's beginnings.

Of course, designing the world's most advanced memory chips puts MOSAID in an ideal position to design and build the engineering systems needed to evaluate them. Testing synchronous memories requires a new approach, for which MOSAID's position is unique: it is the only company to design both the synchronous memories and their testing systems.

MOSAID is also working on specialty memory, in which high-density, standard memo-

ries are combined with added logic circuitry associated with a particular technology. This has major applications in such areas as PC video processing and multimedia. One major development is application specific memory, or ASM. Designed for single applications, such as smart cards, ASM ICs have dramatically higher densities than traditional designs, and will redefine standards for digital electronic products.

MOSAID has invested in ACCELERIX, a semiconductor company which is applying to the multibillion dollar PC market the "systems on a chip" technology that ASM makes possible and that MOSAID predicts will be the foundation of the electronics, multimedia and telecommunications industries by the turn of the century.

MOSAID's Systems Division also focuses on the future, as increasing manufacturing costs force memory chip manufacturers to reduce the size of their chips, and increase storage capacity and processing speed. The Systems Division helps chip manufacturers manage costs and maintain quality by using the unique hardware and software in MOSAID's engineering testers to resolve problems in memory chips. MOSAID's cost-effective designs allow customers to own several MOSAID engineering testers for the price of one production tester, thereby dramatically increasing productivity.

MOSAID's years of leadership in memory design and standardization, its extensive DRAM experience, and its specialization in memory-intensive components all combine to make it the leader in memory design and engineering test systems. The company's vision will define the future beyond SDRAM, into the next century. ■

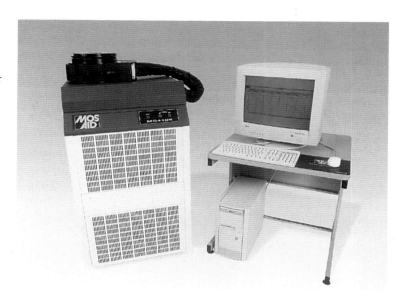

The MOSAID MS4105 Engineering Test System

A portion of the layout for MOSAID's advanced 64M Synchronous Dynamic Random Access Memory (SDRAM) IC memory chip

Bell Mobility

*B*ell Mobility's customers are always in touch.

Bell Mobility, a leader in wireless communications, is one of 15 companies across Canada that make up Mobility Canada, the country's largest provider of cellular and paging services. Bell Mobility serves Quebec and Ontario and operates the world's longest continuous cellular service corridor, stretching over 234,000 square kilometres from Windsor, Ontario, to Sydney, Nova Scotia.

CONVERTO is a two-in-one cordless phone which converts to a cellular.

Add its satellite service, and the range extends from the deserts of New Mexico to Baffin Island and beyond. The satellite covers virtually every square inch of North America, including up to 300 kilometres offshore.

Bell Mobility has invested over a billion dollars in research and development since the company's launch in 1985, and the results speak for themselves. The array of services the company offers surpasses the competition in both variety and quality, and has earned the respect of more than 1.5 million customers in eastern Canada.

Bell Mobility provides those customers with the total spectrum of wireless communications solutions, including cellular, one- and two-way paging, data, satellite and airline passenger communications, as well as the latest technological

breakthrough in Personal Communication Services (PCS).

Whether customers need a mobile office or peace of mind, Bell Mobility offers solutions, along with an understanding that in the years since cellular was first introduced—little more than a decade ago—it has changed the way people work and live. Wireless services are no longer a business luxury but a consumer necessity: for Bell Mobility, they're also about bringing people together—anytime, anywhere.

Technology on the Move

Bell Mobility's Global Roam provides wireless phone service for travellers in over 40 countries. Soon, the company's investment in the Iridium satellite-based phone system, scheduled to begin in 1998, will provide worldwide satellite coverage.

And Bell Mobility's Paging division recently invested $20 million in its new, state-of-the-art Flex network, which provides better message reception and extended battery life. The company's commitment to its customers also includes its Baby Beeper Program, through which expectant parents receive a pager so that loved ones can be notified when the baby is about to arrive.

On the ground or in the air, Bell Mobility doesn't believe in limits. Its digital GenStar phones for airline passenger communications offer the ability to send faxes, use electronic mail and receive calls while in flight. Conference calling capability boosts the value of this service even further, while new signal compression software has meant better quality and reliability in the air.

Bell Mobility solutions are also crossing technology platform barriers. Cellular Data ModemCall allows customers to communicate with any host computer, regardless of the modem on the host side, by linking the call to a wireline system/network. This complements other mobile e-mail options, which enable Bell Mobility customers to create offices that travel wherever they do.

Meanwhile, Message Centre Fax allows customers to move about knowing they will never miss an important fax: documents arrive in an electronic mailbox—just like voice mail—and can be printed to any fax machine or even viewed on a hand-held, pocket-sized display unit.

All of this is offered in the industry's most flexible environment. Bell Mobility's rates are

on average 20 per cent lower than comparable U.S. services, and are offered through imaginative calling options that meet customers' needs, whether they might be integrated packages or individually selected choices. Bell Mobility's bottom line is to provide the most functions at the lowest price, an attitude that keeps its customers satisfied—and coming back.

The combination of advancing technology while maintaining close contact with its users gives an excellent clue as to why the company earned the prestigious "Mercure" award for Company of the Year from the Quebec Chamber of Commerce. And it also explains why more than 25 countries on 5 continents have called on Bell Mobility's expertise to provide consulting services.

The 1995 G-7 summit of leading industrialized nations saw Bell Mobility on hand in Halifax to provide communications support. Working with the summit's official telecom service supplier and Mobility Canada partner, MT&T Mobility, Bell Mobility deployed its mobile cellular station as a back-up for the main cellular network. This transportable cell site, developed by Bell Mobility's Emergency Measures Services group, links cellular and satellite technology for emergency use in almost every environment imaginable.

Safety has always been a high priority for cellular users, many of whom rely on this technology for personal security. Bell Mobility has built partnerships with other organizations, such as radio stations, to extend this vital service. "Star" numbers, for example, provide speed dialling to contact emergency services or to update radio stations on road conditions.

The Road Ahead

Bell Mobility is keeping communications on the move with technological advances that were only dreamed of a few years ago. Imagine for a moment that your phone is no longer just a phone. Now, it's a personal communications device that serves as a residential cordless telephone, office phone, cellular phone, portable computer, pager, and even video monitor.

Science fiction? For Bell Mobility, it's science fact, thanks to the company's work with PCS. The first generation of PCS included familiar analog cellular and paging services; the next generation introduces the digital age.

More than just technology, it's actually a "network of networks" that determines the fastest route on the wireless system to relay information at the lowest possible cost. It links cellular technology with the Internet and multimedia applications, and on its Code Division Multiple Access (CDMA) platform, it will provide a new level of wireless features, including voice, data and video applications.

CDMA, the most widely available digital platform, provides superior voice quality, greater call capacity, fewer dropped or blocked calls, and longer battery life—key advantages to people on the go.

With over a decade of experience, substantial investment in research and technology development, and an attitude that places responsiveness to customers above all else, Bell Mobility will continue breaking down communication barriers.

Just don't ask the company to predict the future: Bell Mobility's too busy inventing it. ∎

Mr. Roy Mlakar, president and CEO of the Ottawa Senators hockey club, is using the Motorola StarTAC cellular phone.

Message Centre Fax allows customers to move about knowing they will never miss an important fax: documents arrive in an electronic mailbox—just like voice mail—and can be printed to any fax machine or even viewed on this hand-held, pocket-sized display unit.

JetForm Corporation

*J*etForm Corporation is the global leader in electronic forms technology. The company's products and solutions streamline the flow of information throughout an organization, from the factory floor to the sales office and the executive suite.

As well as helping corporations to reduce the costs and inefficiencies of processing large quantities of paperwork, electronic forms are now used to change the way a business operates. JetForm builds intelligence into the forms themselves. Fields validate data as it is entered, and automatically perform database checks and calculations. Unlike paper forms, JetForm's unique forms are dynamic. They customize themselves to the data, with sections created instantly as a user enters information. Thus when the data reaches the processing point, it has been validated and is error-free.

JetForm's products can automate the entire life cycle of a business form: they design, fill, route, store, retrieve and deliver the form by way of electronic mail, including the Internet. The modular software can be mixed, matched or customized to perform all the tasks a particular organization requires.

One of the fast-growing companies in the Ottawa-Carleton region, JetForm evolved from a small, regional software consulting firm to become the largest developer of electronic forms software in the world. The company's beginnings date to 1981, when this region was becoming known as a spawning ground for fledgling advanced technology firms. JetForm was founded by a group of four individuals who had been involved in other successful high-tech start-ups, and pioneered forms automation.

In the late 1980s, JetForm's founders (who remain active in the company) invited entrepreneur and former colleague John Kelly to join the company as a director and to help map out its future. Under the guidance of Mr. Kelly, who was subsequently appointed president and then chief executive officer, JetForm carved out its present niche. By 1997, JetForm had over 500 employees and filled the high-rise office building of which, 15 years earlier, it occupied a corner suite.

Proud of its Ottawa roots, JetForm plays a leadership role in the region's civic and professional organizations, and is a generous financial supporter of community charities and sports associations. JetForm fixed its logo to the Ottawa skyline by stepping up to the plate as corporate sponsor of Ottawa's baseball stadium. JetForm Park is home to the Triple A Ottawa Lynx.

In the highly competitive software business, however, JetForm is unquestionably in the major leagues. When forms automation moved into the industrial mainstream in the mid-1990s, JetForm aggressively extended its market reach through acquisitions, alliances with major international software developers and expansion into new markets. The company has established offices and distributorships in Canada and the United States, Latin America, Europe, Scandinavia, the Asia-Pacific region and China to serve corporations around the globe.

JetForm's most significant boost to its growth was the acquisition of its major competitor, the Delrina Group, in 1996. Toronto-based Delrina had become a subsidiary of Symantec Corporation of Cupertino, California. By bringing Delrina into its own corporate fold, JetForm acquired full ownership of all of Delrina's electronic business forms-related products, as well

JetForm headquarters, Ottawa, Ontario Canada

JetForm fixed its logo to the Ottawa skyline by stepping up to the plate as corporate sponsor of Ottawa's baseball stadium. JetForm Park is home to the Triple A Ottawa Lynx.

as the firm's research and development talent. Delrina's R&D team has remained intact in Toronto, while marketing staff moved to Ottawa headquarters.

Other acquisitions have included Proactive Systems of England, a European leader in developing electronic forms, and Eclipse Corporation of Atlanta, Georgia. Eclipse is known for its award-winning IBM AS/400 electronic forms. Since the IBM AS/400 is among the most popular multi-use computing systems worldwide, the Eclipse buyout has dramatically increased JetForm's market penetration. As a result of these and the Delrina acquisitions, JetForm effectively captured 80 per cent of the world market in business forms automation.

A major JetForm strategy is tailoring its products to complement and add value to software produced by industry leaders like Microsoft, SAP, IBM, UNISYS, Sun Microsystems, PC Docs and Hewlett-Packard. IBM and UNISYS, for example, have integrated JetForm electronic forms with their banking packages. Hewlett-Packard, the world leader in laser printers, sells a laser printer with JetForm software already programmed into it. This ensures very high speed production, since the forms don't have to recreated each time they're needed.

In Europe, JetForm has collaborated with SAP AG of Germany, a leading software developer with a highly sophisticated, complex system that ties together and automates the basic processes of business from taking orders to balancing the books. With JetForm Central™ software, customers can form-enable their SAP™ applications, creating high-quality printed forms ranging from invoices to packing lists. Because of this relationship, JetForm products serve SAP customers throughout Europe and North America, including many U.S.-based multinational corporations.

JetForm is an innovator committed to capturing new market opportunities like the World Wide Web. The Web has created a global electronic marketplace that is changing the way many companies do business, and JetForm was the first electronic forms developer to launch products that are usable on the Web. With JetForm software, a company can cut the time and cost of processing business transactions between enterprises. It can also develop new sources of business. A major Canadian bank was first on the Web with JetForm-engineered interactive software to attract

mortgage customers.

Banks, insurance companies, health care organizations, law enforcement agencies and government, all heavily dependent on administrative procedures and forms, are key JetForm customers. JetForm uses the customer's own information technology infrastructure—such as local area networks, e-mail systems and databases—to integrate electronic forms with the organizational workflow.

JetForm's FormFlow™, for example, has been adopted by over three-quarters of all Canadian government departments. The federal government's human resources branch saves some $1.4 million every year by using FormFlow to streamline the processing of 800 different forms. In addition to eliminating printing and mailing costs, FormFlow has sped up approvals dramatically while reducing clerical and administrative work.

In a rapidly expanding market, JetForm is poised to seize new opportunities and establish JetForm technology as the de facto standard for electronic forms and administrative workflow solutions. ■

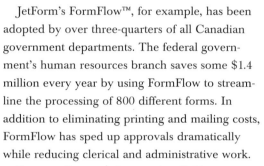

John Kelly, JetForm president and CEO

JetForm is an innovator committed to capturing new market opportunities like the World Wide Web. The Web has created a global electronic marketplace that is changing the way many companies do business, and JetForm was the first electronic forms developer to launch products that are usable on the Web.

i-STAT Corporation

i-STAT Corporation is a global leader in developing unique blood-testing devices for medical use. An international company with offices in Kanata, Ontario, and in Princeton, New Jersey, i-STAT develops, manufactures and markets the world's first, hand-held blood analyzer.

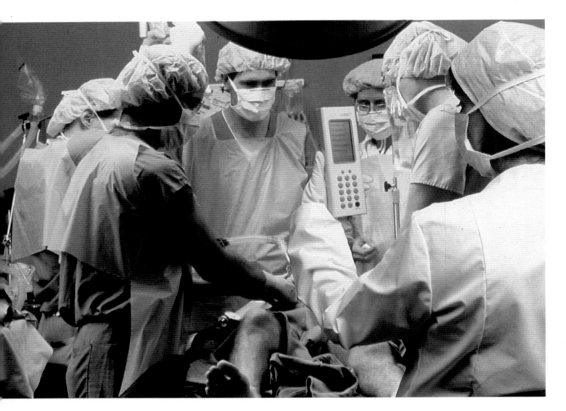

i-STAT critical care instrument provides fast turnaround results for patient care.

Less than two minutes after testing a few drops of a patient's blood in the analyzer, the physician or nurse can determine blood oxygen levels and other important chemical balances in the patient's bloodstream. Sparing the expense and turnaround time of sending blood samples to a laboratory, i-STAT's computerized analyzer allows the physician to obtain test results, then prescribe medical treatment for a critically ill patient without leaving the bedside.

Its simple design, ease of use and reliability have won kudos from medical staff, and the i-STAT system is finding a ready market in hospital emergency, intensive care, neonatal nursery and kidney dialysis units throughout North America and Europe. Paramedics, home-care agencies, outpatient surgery centres and veterinarians also use the device. Because of its portability, the analyzer is especially useful in situations where turnaround speed is essential and there is no access to laboratory facilities. It has been adopted by medical staff

in disaster relief clinics, army field hospitals and navy submarines, on holiday cruise liners and NASA's space shuttle missions.

Imants R. Lauks, i-STAT executive vice-president and originator of the cutting-edge technology, says the time is opportune for the product. "In the restructuring of health-care delivery and the effort to reduce costs, our mission is to provide new solutions and set new standards in blood analysis. The i-STAT system gives clinicians the ability to perform laboratory tests without leaving the patient's side."

In fact, the i-STAT system makes blood analysis as easy and routine as taking a patient's temperature. It simply requires two or three drops of blood to be placed into the disposable test cartridge, which is then inserted into the battery-operated analyzer. Results are displayed in 90 seconds, and records are automatically stored for later review, printing or electronic transfer to the hospital's information system. Each unit can store up to 50 patient records, so it can be used for extended periods without interruption.

At the heart of i-STAT's blood analyzer is an innovative melding of microelectronics with biochemical and silicon chip technologies. Much as silicon chips propelled personal computer technology, advances in silicon biosensors enabled i-STAT's blood-testing device. "Our system achieves previously unattainable miniaturization of sophisticated components. The result is a highly accurate, truly portable blood analyzer that contains many of the basic analytical subsystems found in a laboratory," Lauks says.

Different sensor configurations in the cartridges enable clinicians to test for a wide range of blood chemicals that provide crucial medical information. For example, a blood glucose test can reveal diabetes or show if insulin treatments are correct. A test of chloride levels helps to monitor how well the kidneys and respiratory systems are working. The speed and accuracy of the i-STAT analyzer are particularly important when a patient is too ill to respond to a physician's questions yet needs urgent treatment. The company's research and development effort is focused on adding to the range of blood tests the i-STAT system can perform.

Imants Lauks founded i-STAT Corporation in 1983 to refine and market the biochemical silicon chip technology he had developed while a professor at the University of Pennsylvania. In 1988, the company's original base of operations in

Princeton, New Jersey, was augmented by research and manufacturing facilities in Ottawa-Carleton because of the silicon chip fabrication experience in this region. The i-STAT system was brought to market in 1992. By 1997, the company had a staff of over 450 professional and support staff on both sides of the Canada-United States border. Marketing and sales are conducted from Princeton, while the technical and manufacturing expertise remain in Kanata. i-STAT is a publicly owned company and its shares trade on the U.S. NASDAQ exchange.

Industry alliances are an important aspect of the company's growth strategy. In the mid-1990s, i-STAT forged a partnership with the Hewlett-Packard Company, the world market leader in manufacturing and selling vital signs monitoring equipment. As part of this collaboration, teams from both companies are integrating i-STAT technology into HP's patient-monitoring products such as the Omnicare System, which is installed at bedsides around the world. With HP, i-STAT will expand its international markets in the United States, Europe, Africa, the Middle East and the countries that were part of the former Soviet Union. As well, i-STAT has separate marketing alliances in Japan and South America.

While its market reach is global, i-STAT is a committed supporter of professional and civic organizations in the Ottawa-Carleton region. In collaboration with local business development organizations and educational institutions, the company is helping to ensure that there are skilled workers to sustain the region's advanced technology industries into the future. As a member of the Ottawa-Carleton Manufacturers Managers

Challenges for i-STAT testing on the space shuttle included holding on to the instrument.

Network, i-STAT worked to pioneer a local apprenticeship program in microelectronics skills in conjunction with Algonquin College. The company also cooperates with Carleton University and the University of Ottawa in training process engineers and other technologists for the region's burgeoning technology sector.

"As an organization, our growth will be realized through the development and enhancement of our employees' skills," Lauks says. "We want to excel as a learning organization, ensuring that employees have support for developing their expertise." Similarly, i-STAT extends this support to the Ottawa-Carleton community. "People with appropriate technical backgrounds—the key to the survival and growth of this economy is human resources." ■

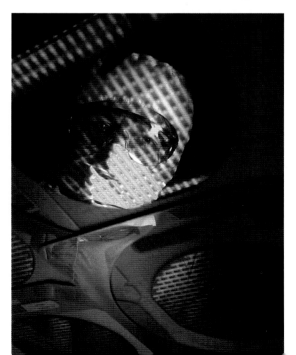

Manufacturing i-STAT sensors requires working in a clean room environment using similar techniques as computer chip suppliers.

SPS Computing and Engineering and Bradson Staffing Inc.

Strength in versatility. It's more than SPS Computing and Engineering's motto: it's the foundation of the company's success. Now a subsidiary of Bradson Staffing Inc.,

**The Bradson Business Centre—
Committed to Business**

SPS has served Ottawa's high-technology community since 1969, specializing in the staffing of computing and engineering contracts.

Originally founded around the research and development of a high-tech instrument to measure the density of liquids, SPS has leveraged the computerization of society into a business focused not simply on technology, but on the minds that drive it. Through responsiveness has come growth.

Using a leading-edge database of qualified professionals who possess the right level of technical skills and industry exposure, SPS is able to consistently offer profitable information technology solutions within 48 hours of the client's request.

SPS provides skilled personnel in system design and development, information technology management, technical support and computer services centred around an extensive range of hardware platforms and software disciplines.

This approach has enabled SPS to gain vast application experience in such sectors as government, utilities, banking, aerospace, insurance and health care. Constant innovation and a high ethical standard have ensured its continued growth and globalization.

It has also meant a world of difference to local high-tech firms and government, to be provided with the human resources talent needed to enable sophisticated projects to succeed.

A Global Perspective

Keeping pace with global development, SPS operates in all three NAFTA countries and has successfully completed worldwide projects for its clients in locations as varied as Romania, Switzerland, Korea and Hawaii in addition to Canada, the U.S. and Mexico.

Wherever it operates, SPS sets itself apart by doing the job right, the first time. Its flexibility has proven its reputation repeatedly, even on its Hawaii operation, where an SPS employee arrived to discover that the assignment, involving telescope electronics, was in the middle of a snow belt, atop a mountain!

On the Home Front

The company is also active here in Ottawa, with executives serving on many civic committees, including the Kidney Foundation, Cancer Society, Big Brothers Association, Opera Lyra Ottawa and the United Way. Bradson encourages its staff to participate in community events outside the organization, such as the annual H.O.P.E. Beach Volleyball Tournament.

Extension into the community is natural for Bradson, being 100-percent Canadian-owned and headquartered in Ottawa. For more than 40 years, it has served its community, at home and abroad, in the vanguard of the staffing industry.

Matching People and Opportunities

When Stanley Arron founded Bradson in 1957, the company was the first staffing agency in Ottawa. A small firm in the early days providing clerical and office administration services, Bradson has since expanded into a full-service staffing agency with specialties in the areas of office support, industrial and skilled trades, electronic assembly, professional, technical, home health care, security and call centre staffing services.

The company is one of the largest privately owned suppliers of temporary, permanent and contract staffing services in Canada, with clients who rely on it for cost-effective personnel solutions.

Throughout its history, Bradson has watched market trends and listened to its customers in order to develop its services. The staffing industry itself is one of the fastest growing in North America, a result of the huge shift in the employment environment, while technological expansion has added further staffing pressures to many sectors.

Bradson's understanding of the need to minimize business costs while using the best human resources has led it to offer the largest range of services and options in the industry. It can assist with permanent, temporary and temporary-to-permanent staffing, contract staffing of entire projects or specific project team positions, payrolling, blended staffing for help during seasonal busy periods, and turn-key outsourcing (where the company staffs and manages an entire support function).

Through both internal growth and external acquisitions, Bradson has strengthened its service

lines and responded to its customers. The purchase of SPS in 1996 complemented Bradson's existing strength in the information technology field. The 1997 acquisition of a Seattle high-tech staffing company added a West Coast presence to SPS.

Growth has also come through Bradson and SPS clients. For those needing services in a new location, or on a national scale, the company goes with them, operating on location to ensure the exacting standard of service that clients have come to expect from the Bradson organization.

Customer requests have also led to expansions within, and the addition of new service lines. As an example, Bradson's Tele-Staffing Services, established in 1995, offers specialized staffing solutions specifically tailored to the call centre industry, a burgeoning sector of the national economy.

The Bradson Advantage

People are the Bradson and SPS advantage. Bradson recruits the most capable, enthusiastic, creative employees possible, providing clients with premier service, excellent resources, discerning consultants and innovative approaches.

While companies benefit from the specific focus of Bradson's departmentalized service lines, all the lines and companies work closely together to deliver a full range of services. Client satisfaction is assured through uniform high quality, a single service entry point for all staffing requirements and the strength of the Bradson organization.

Bradson's ISO 9002 certification in a number of its divisions and service lines reflects the company's commitment to quality. Other divisions, including SPS, are currently going through the certification process.

With more than 40 years of proven staffing services experience, and 25 years of strong information technology performance, Bradson Staffing Inc. and SPS Computing and Engineering offer their clients efficient, economical, exceptional services—no matter where they operate. An Ottawa-based success story! ∎

Corporate Citation

Certificat auprès des entreprises

SPS

Thank you! Merci!
for your corporate contribution to this year's campaign.
pour votre don corporatif offert à la campagne de cette année.

Peter Cleveland
Campaign Chair/Président de la campagne
United Way/Centraide Ottawa-Carleton
1996

People Helping People   Un geste qui compte

Committed to the Ottawa Community

KPMG

Certificate of Registration

This is to certify that KPMG Quality Registrar has registered the Quality System of

Bradson Staffing Services

440 Laurier Avenue West, Ottawa, Ontario K1R 7X6

to the Quality System Standard

ISO 9002:1994

The Quality System is applicable to

Temporary, permanent and contract staffing of office support, administrative and sales positions

This registration is given subject to the terms and conditions governing the use of this certificate as described in the agreement between KPMG Quality Registrar Inc. and the holder thereof. Registration does not assure the effectiveness of the Quality System or the products or services produced by it.

Certificate Number: 045
Issue Date: October 18, 1995
Expiration Date: October 17, 1998

Mark J. O'Sullivan
President
KPMG Quality Registrar Inc.

Committed to Excellence and Quality

MDS Nordion

MDS Nordion, Ottawa-Carleton's largest health and life sciences company, is a world leader in radioisotope technology. It exports 95 per cent of its sales to over 70 countries, with many of its valuable products able to reach their markets within an astounding 24 hours of their production.

But the company, which makes products to improve the life and health of millions of people worldwide, has its roots firmly planted in Ottawa-Carleton.

These roots are seen in MDS Nordion's involvement with community projects in Kanata, the community where many of its employees live and work, and in the company's assistance to Ottawa-area health care facilities such as the Women's Breast Health Centre at the Ottawa Civic Hospital.

MDS Nordion has come a long way. When Roy Errington founded the company in Ottawa in 1946, its focus was marketing radium. But by 1951, the company had installed the world's first commercial cobalt 60 cancer therapy unit, and in 1954 it sold its first Gammacell® laboratory research irradiator—still in use today. It launched the commercial production of molybdenum 99, for which it now provides most of the world's supply, in 1972.

In 1991, the entrepreneurial spirit and international perspective that fuelled both the company's growth and its advancement of radioisotope and irradiation technology led it to join MDS Inc., the largest Canadian-based health and life sciences firm.

It's a natural fit. The company's products and services are used by health care providers to diagnose and treat disease. They are also used to prevent the spread of disease by providing manufacturers of medical and surgical products with a safe, effective method of sterilization.

Every year, roughly 20 million diagnostic imaging tests are carried out around the world.

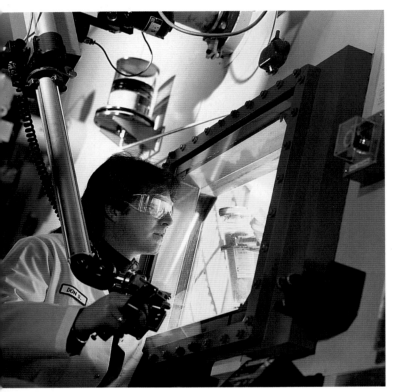

MDS Nordion's global vision has made it a world leader with markets in over 70 countries.

MDS Nordion has the experience and resources, technical and human, to develop new applications for radioisotope technology.

MDS Nordion's radioisotopes are the principal elements in the products used for these nuclear medicine procedures. Bone scans, heart studies and thyroid imaging all use isotopes. Radioisotopes also have some therapeutic applications.

MDS Nordion markets the radioisotope cobalt 60 and designs and installs the sterilization systems that use this isotope as a source of gamma radiation. Gamma radiation passes through materials, destroying dangerous bacteria without affecting the product or leaving harmful residue. This technology is ideal for treating disposable medical supplies, cosmetics and other consumer products. It is also a highly effective method of killing bacteria that cause food-borne illness and food spoilage.

Gamma energy is also harnessed in MDS Nordion's smaller Gammacell® and research irradiators. Gammacells® are used by hospitals and blood banks to treat blood for patients with severely weakened immune systems who are vulnerable to graft versus host disease, which is fatal.

MDS Nordion is continually developing new products and applications that will improve the health and quality of life of people around the world. For instance, they have demonstrated how gamma radiation can turn sewage into safe fertilizer. They are also dedicated to developing new products for the early detection and treatment of cancer and other diseases. For example, TheraSphere®, an innovative alternative to traditional methods of treating liver cancer, was approved in 1991 for sale in Canada.

MDS Nordion is a subsidiary of MDS Inc., with headquarters in Toronto. MDS products and services meet the needs of three customer groups: health care providers, manufacturers of medical and life science products and health care consumers. ∎

Computing Devices Canada

**Reconnaissance Vehicle
Surveillance System (RVSS)**

Computing Devices Canada, or CDC, has a global reputation for delivering innovative and high-value systems, software and hardware. From NATO to the Pacific Rim, from industry to the armed forces of more than 20 countries, CDC's high performance technology-based solutions cover everything from land mine detection to shipboard sonars.

In an industry where systems are often mission critical, CDC responds with technology of superior strength and reliability, thanks to the company's continuous investment in customer-driven research and development. Through the complete product life cycle, from concept to post-delivery support, CDC's unique expertise includes project management, comprehensive manufacturing and full logistic capacity.

CDC was established in 1948, and is an independently operating member of the Ceridian group of companies. In its 50 years, the company has produced a number of world firsts and exciting technological breakthroughs.

In explaining its success, CDC describes itself as an engineering company with a heavy systems engineering bent, a company in which developing software doesn't mean sitting in one place and writing lines of code. Employees work closely with customers, talking first-hand with the operators of the end system, learning about the customer's environment, their needs, and the capabilities and constraints that must be met.

In often lengthy development cycles, the close relationship between CDC and its customers provides real value to both, as each becomes an essential part of the other's team, focused on a common purpose.

This has translated into an overwhelming 98 per cent of respondents to CDC's most recent customer survey stating that they would welcome doing business with CDC again. The numbers reflect CDC's total quality management approach and its system of integrated product development, which creates one team for each project. The customer is a key player on the team, which brings together all company departments working on the project to form a powerful, cohesive unit.

These approaches create an entrepreneurial feel to the company at every level. Technology interchanges with other CDC locations and the Ceridian group add to this, ensuring lively exchanges of ideas and perspective, the effective sharing of technology advances and the building of economies of scale—all of which help create cost-efficient, low-risk results for CDC's customers.

Close relationships with several major universities and colleges complement CDC's own cutting-edge research and development efforts.

A survey of the resulting achievements is impressive: The world's first digital fire control system, first applied on the Abrams M1 Tank. Leading militarized Electroluminescent Flat Panel Displays. MESHnet—a state-of-the-art, integrated, secure tactical communications technology. And unmatched expertise in integrating "off-the-shelf" technology into the military environment, as in the Light Armoured Vehicle Reconnaissance Surveillance System.

From its emphasis on software reliability to its use of Hoshin Planning to ensure that the company's objectives are linked throughout its departments, Computing Devices Canada continues to build on its half-century of stability, while consistently pushing the forward edges of technology. It's advanced electronics for today… and tomorrow. ■

Computing Devices Canada, Ottawa

Northern Micro

*K*een entrepreneurial sense, a solid knowledge of the market, top-quality products and outstanding customer service have helped founder Herman Yeh to boost Northern Micro into the leagues of Canada's 100 fastest growing companies. Between 1992 and 1996, the company's sales exploded from $2.6 million to $36.7 million.

Northern Micro's high level of manufacturing quality earned the company ISO 9002 certification.

Northern Micro specializes in customizing computer equipment for government and corporate offices, focusing on personal computer systems and servers that meet exacting international technical standards as well as clients' specific needs.

"Northern Micro can design, configure and deliver exactly the system our clients require. As an independent supplier we are free to mix and match technologies. The result is that we provide fresh solutions to the never-ending demand for more speed, more stability, better value," Yeh says.

In addition to its Ottawa-Carleton headquarters, Northern Micro has offices in Vancouver, Halifax and Quebec City. The company is also supported by a national network of service contractors to handle troubleshooting coast-to-coast and around the clock.

Northern Micro Computer

A computer scientist educated at the University of Toronto, Yeh was an information technology specialist with the federal public service when he left to launch Northern Micro in 1985. Yeh remains its president and driving force, and since the early 1990s has carved out a market niche supplying large federal government agencies like Statistics Canada with customized network equipment. Members of Parliament and their House of Commons staff are also users of Northern Micro equipment.

Yeh says his company thrives by keeping abreast of new technological developments that will benefit clients, and by offering quality service at competitive prices. "An efficient network environment requires 100 per cent unit dependability as well as absolute continuity and consistency in equipment design," he comments. "It then requires creativity and solid technical expertise. We are reliable, innovative and flexible."

Although Northern Micro's major clients are federal government departments in the Ottawa-Hull area, the company has been expanding its market to include municipal governments and companies outside the region, and multinational corporations like Bell Northern Research (BNR) and Newbridge Corporation. Yeh explains that an advanced technology manufacturer like Newbridge has to run tests for its products on a battery of personal computers, and so has called on Northern Micro to put together the PC systems for this purpose since 1995. Similarly, Northern serves the computer experts in BNR's engineering laboratories.

Northern delivers both local- and wide-area networking solutions. Installations can include workstations, servers, network cards, cabling, concentrators and network and application software.

In its own manufacturing facility, Northern Micro assembles its products under the Spirit trademark, using top-quality, name-brand components such as Intel, Quantum, Western Digital, IBM, ATI, ADI and Panasonic. Northern's high level of manufacturing quality earned the company ISO 9002 certification, given by the International Standards Organization only to products that meet stringent specifications when subjected to rigorous, independent tests. The company is also recognized by the Government of Canada as a Circle Canada-certified manufacturer, one of a world-class elite. ∎

Nortel

Nortel (Northern Telecom) has translated high technology into high energy in the Ottawa-Carleton region since 1958, when the company (then known as Northern Electric) chose a site just west of Canada's national capital for a central laboratory.

Now among the world's leading telecommunications research and development facilities, Nortel's Ottawa complexes form a strategic component of the company's global operations, which span 150 countries and some 68,000 employees.

In 1996, Nortel invested $2.5 billion Canadian in R&D worldwide—approximately 14 per cent of its revenues. Roughly half was spent in Canada, and of that, the company's Ottawa-region facilities handled more than 92 per cent.

Nortel renewed its commitment to the region in 1997, with plans to increase its workforce by 5,000 employees over four years to a total of 15,000. With more than 10,000 employees, Nortel was already Ottawa-Carleton's largest private-sector employer.

"Nortel is Canada's flagship high-technology company and the centrepiece of Ottawa's internationally renowned community," notes Gedas Sakus, president, technology at Nortel. "Nortel is expanding in the Ottawa region because it is the high-tech centre of Canada. The talent we can attract to Ottawa is allowing us to win in international markets."

Nortel operates in four main lines of business that, among them, comprise 38 independent business units, each headed by a general manager. Ottawa undertakes advanced R&D for all of the lines of business at its 16 locations in the region and is home to several key business units.

Poised for significant growth to accommodate Nortel's expansion, the Carling site at Moodie Drive and Carling Avenue is Nortel's largest research and product development location, encompassing more than 1.3 million square feet. With five labs, including one of the most sophisticated clean-room facilities in the world, Carling is home to designers, developers, scientists and technicians working in such areas as terminal design, global enterprise services, optoelectronic devices, and very high-speed integrated circuits. It also houses the Advanced Components organization, which explores, develops and manufactures semiconductors and other components that make key contributions to the success of Nortel products.

In fact, Nortel is home to a growing number of strategically important businesses, including global data communications (such as the Magellan portfolio of data and broadband multimedia networking products), and Entrust, a leading provider of information security products.

The company has found key advantages in locating—and expanding—in Ottawa-Carleton: the region's high quality of life attracts employees, as does the fact that Ottawa has become the high-tech nerve of the country. Traditionally, Nortel in Ottawa has been known for R&D. With the expansion, however, comes an emphasis on other critical business processes, such as marketing, product planning and business development.

"We value this country as a great place to do business," says Nortel president and chief operating officer John Roth. "As the future unfolds, and as Nortel expands globally, we will also continue to grow Canada's reputation—and Ottawa-Carleton's—as a centre of global expertise in communications." ■

A design engineer preparing to evaluate the acoustic performance of a Nortel wireless handset on a head and torso simulator in Nortel's anechoic chamber.

A scientist in Nortel's Advanced Technology Laboratory using a secondary ion mass spectrometry system to investigate optoelectronic devices and very high-speed integrated circuits.

Quatrosense Environmental Limited

The corporate mission of Quatrosense Environmental Limited (QEL) doesn't pull any punches. Committed to protecting life, property and the environment, QEL's focus on quality and reliability hallmarks every facet of the company's operations. QEL designs, manufactures and services an innovative array of instrumentation primarily focused on the monitoring and control of emissions, environmental pollutants and industrial contaminants.

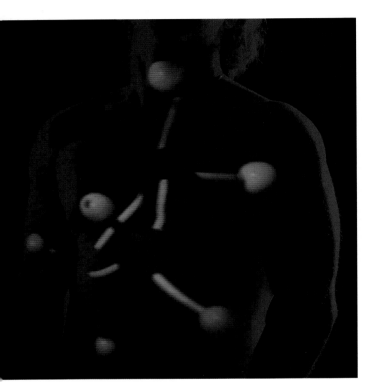

David Jenkins saw the potential of this field in 1986, when he founded QEL with a mandate to increase the level of technological development in the gas detection industry. QEL's first product, which monitors vehicle exhaust in parking garages, received rapid acceptance in the commercial building market, securing approximately 75 per cent of new construction business by 1990.

That year marked QEL's purchase of RAB Dedesco, a 20-year-old, Ottawa-based manufacturer of portable and fixed combustion analyzers with a well-established name for providing rugged, reliable equipment. QEL also moved from Nepean to Richmond in 1990, into a custom-built 18,000-square-foot facility that houses the combined operations.

Since 1991, QEL has diversified its product line, operating in five key areas: hazardous gas detection, optical flame detection, combustion analyzers, site services and packaged systems. As a result, QEL equipment now operates through a broad spectrum: from mining, petrochemical brewing, and pulp and paper facilities to chemical and food processing plants, recreational buildings and landfills.

Increasingly, customers call upon QEL's skills in developing custom equipment and complete, packaged systems. In one recent project, turned around in a revolutionary six weeks, QEL developed sensors to meet the requirements of kraft pulp mills to detect substantially lower levels of chlorine dioxide. In another, the company created an ammonia sensor that could operate in freezer conditions, below the temperature limits of existing technology.

QEL's new technology centre, where software, mechanical and electronics engineering jointly develop custom applications, enables the company to provide customers with technological solutions.

Nowhere is this more apparent than in QEL's groundbreaking work in the brewing industry, designing, installing and servicing a packaged system that uses digital technology to monitor gas emissions and transmit results to a central data acquisition system.

QEL solicits feedback directly from customers in order to provide products that fulfil the needs of the real people who will use and maintain them. But the company takes this one step further: QEL also gives key distributors and customers the opportunity to participate in preliminary design specifications and test prototype products, and it works closely with customers to develop new technologies, as it did in the brewery project. This company-wide attention to the needs of others is reflected in QEL's monthly donations to a selected list of local and national causes, such as Heart and Stroke, Juvenile Diabetes, Ottawa Boys and Girls Club and local Goulbourn concerns.

It's another example of the driving force that has made QEL the sixth largest manufacturer of gas detection equipment in North America: the concern for people, for the success of its customers and for the environment. ■

QEL both detects and protects! The cyclo-propane molecule superimposed over the chest of a healthy individual depicts the relationship between early gas detection and the ultimate protection of health and equipment. Photo by Ari Tapiero.

Research and development have produced high-tech solutions to real world problems. Photo by Ari Tapiero.

CHAPTER THIRTEEN

The Business Community

Ernst & Young

*E*rnst & Young has served the Ottawa-Carleton community for more than 50 years, providing the highest quality business advice to clients ranging from start-up phase to well-established corporations. Located in the downtown core, the team of 130 dedicated professionals offers a full range of advisory services to high technology, public sector organizations, individuals and companies in many industries.

Ernst & Young's Ottawa team draws from its Canada-wide resources in all major business centres. Their nationwide professional staff of 3,700 is expert in areas of business process improvement, information technology, international tax, business consulting, insolvency, accounting and auditing, and Canadian taxation. As well, the firm offers actuarial, benefits and compensation services, forensic accounting and litigation support.

Barbara Tuttle and a client contemplating Research and Development tax planning

Through Ernst & Young International, global clients enjoy not only access to vast business knowledge, but also a network of extensive business and government connections. Ernst & Young International is comprised of 60,000 professionals located in 140 countries, serving more multinational corporations than any other business advisory firm.

As business environments change, Ernst & Young is in the forefront of anticipating client needs. "Clients, whether rapid growth entrepreneurial companies or long-established corporations, seek business advice that goes far beyond accounting and auditing," observed Peter Cleveland, managing partner of Ernst & Young's Ottawa office.

Cleveland speaks from the perspective of 25 years as a professional advisor in financial reorganizations and strategic planning. As a senior Ernst & Young partner, he, together with his Ottawa professional team, are driving strong growth for the firm. "Innovative solutions, designed to promote client growth, stability and profitability, are the cornerstone of Ernst & Young services," he said. "As well, our audit approach is shifting away from transactional verification toward assessing business risks and identifying creative solutions to help clients meet their goals."

Located close to the heart of Canada's thriving high-technology sector, Ernst & Young serves the region's fast-growing software, manufacturing and telecommunications companies. The firm offers clients a solid track record, advising many of the most successful high-technology companies in both Canada and the United States. Ernst & Young is an advisor and auditor to more than 30 per cent of the top-ranked North American electronics companies and the top 50 independent software developers. In recent years, the firm has assisted more than half those Silicon Valley companies that have realized their initial public share offerings.

Whether a company is in a start-up or expansion mode, growth poses special challenges, often stretching its people, systems and financing. Using a team approach, Ernst & Young specialists assist companies to successfully develop opportunities—creating value for shareholders. This may include facilitating a strategic direction nationally and internationally, or involve locating strategic partners, taking the company public or devising a plan to lower its overall tax rate.

For companies poised to enter new markets, Ernst & Young offers extensive support concerning all aspects of business environments, market surveys and feasibility studies, introduction of potential business partners, advice on corporate structure and joint ventures.

Peter Cleveland, Managing Partner

Government agencies and other public sector organizations have their own challenging needs. In these times of an ever-shrinking public purse, taxpayers demand greater efficiency, better accountability and improved results. Above all, public agencies must do more with less. Ernst & Young's leadership in process improvement makes it a logical choice for the public sector.

The firm's audit innovation initiatives provide not only audit assurance, but also opportunities for improving key management and operational processes–supporting client profitability goals. As well, using its extensive best practices knowledge base, Ernst & Young benchmarks the strengths and weaknesses of client operations against those of peer organizations within each industry–helping clients to implement process improvements.

Ernst & Young's Corporate Recovery & Insolvency Group offers a full range of professional debt restructuring, financial review and formal insolvency services. The group offers services in both large corporate and mid-sized company markets.

In recent years, businesses and their advisors have had to deal with an increasingly wider range of financial issues. Accurate analysis and interpretation of financial information is absolutely critical to formulate effective solutions to complex business problems. Ernst & Young's Forensic Accounting and Litigation Support Group provides investigative services to the legal profession, the corporate sector, regulatory organizations and law enforcement agencies.

Providing excellent tax advice has always been a core Ernst & Young service. Today, the firm has the largest group of tax experts in the world, offering both comprehensive and specialized tax planning. Ernst & Young professionals have in-depth knowledge of all special tax situations in Canada and abroad–including commodity and expatriate taxes, beneficial investment structures and special purpose institutions such as banks and insurance companies.

The Ottawa office is an integral part of the firm's international tax network. The tax team diligently develops innovative tax strategies–

Left to right: Partners Steve Pittman, Michael Connolly, Peter Cleveland, Mario Clément

Left to right: Mylène Levac-Wolf (Audit), Peter Cleveland (Strategic Planning), Robert Fonberg (Management Consulting), and Jay Humphrey (Tax), form a client service team focus.

whether relating to financing, acquisitions or research and development–tailored to ensure clients fulfill their long-range business objectives.

The essence of Ernst & Young is its people. The firm recruits and retains high-performance individuals, dedicated to the best interests of clients. They care about their communities, and volunteerism is an important part of the firm's culture. Partners in the Ottawa office are volunteer directors or financial advisors to more than 20 community organizations and projects.

In support of excellence in business, the firm co-sponsors Profit 100, a national award given to the fastest growing companies in Canada. Ernst & Young also co-sponsors the Canada-wide Entrepreneur of the Year program, designed to recognize successful business entrepreneurs.

With its Canadian and international expertise, Ernst & Young offers a unique wealth of resources to help clients tackle their business challenges. ■

Nesbitt Burns

Nesbitt Burns, a member of the Bank of Montreal Group of Companies, has a clear objective: to be the premier Canadian investment firm in Canada. Its Ottawa operation shows just how to achieve that: it's the largest full-service investment firm in the area, with the most investment advisors of any investment dealer in the city. Branches in outlying communities extend the company's coverage throughout eastern Ontario and western Quebec.

But success means more to Nesbitt Burns than numbers. It means people.

The merger of two of Canada's leading investment firms in 1994—Nesbitt Thomson Inc. and Burns Fry Limited—created Nesbitt Burns, and imbued it with over 250 combined years of experience in building and preserving wealth for generations of clients.

Today, its four offices in Ottawa offer over 90 investment advisors, backed by a company-wide strength of more than 3,500 dedicated professionals. For the investment needs of individuals and corporations to those of governments and institutions, Nesbitt Burns provides a depth of resources second to none in the Canadian investment industry, including the top-rated research department in Canada.

Working Together

Nesbitt Burns understands that investing can appear complex and time-consuming. By providing individual, personalized service, the firm steps between its clients and the vast array of investment decisions, offering advice that responds to each situation.

An immediate appointment with an investment advisor is only the beginning. The advisors work with their

clients to understand their financial goals, develop an appropriate investment plan and create customized investment portfolios that match the clients' objectives.

Each plan is tailored to fit short- and long-term goals, risk tolerance levels and the amount of time the client wishes to spend monitoring and managing the portfolio. The plan's overall intention, which might involve saving for retirement, building an education fund or managing a business for growth, always remains the key focus.

Nesbitt Burns believes in a balanced, portfolio approach to investment. Mutual funds, equity investments and fixed income assets; foreign investments, new issues and retirement options—the firm has the products and services to support whatever its clients need. Nesbitt Burns also offers specialized, innovative accounts with the most accessible minimum investment levels of the industry, plus investment management, insurance and estate planning services.

Reaching Out

Nesbitt Burns' belief in service includes its community. The company's objective—to be the best at everything it does—applies equally here. Whether it's behind the scenes or in front of the cameras, the Ottawa offices believe strongly in giving back to the region in which they make their living.

Groups such as the Ottawa Civic Hospital Foundation and its Heart Institute Telethon, the Children's Hospital of Eastern Ontario, the Royal Ottawa Hospital, Easter Seals and the Rotary Club have come to rely on the energy and dedication of the firm's staff.

That's just the way Nesbitt Burns does business—personal, committed and working together to reach common goals. ■

Today, the four offices of Nesbitt Burns in Ottawa offer over 90 investment advisors, backed by a company-wide strength of more than 3,500 dedicated professionals. For the investment needs of individuals and corporations to those of governments and institutions, Nesbitt Burns provides a depth of resources second to none in the Canadian investment industry.

Nationwide, the Bank of Montreal shares almost $17 million a year with charities and through various sponsorships. This strength in community life comes in part from its network of more than 1,200 bank branches located across the country and in key locations around the world.

Bank of Montreal

Bank of Montreal maintains a bold presence in Ottawa's downtown core, with its main branch overlooking Parliament Hill on one side and forming part of Sparks Street Mall on the other side. From its regional headquarters in the heart of the city to its 26 locations serving Ottawa-Carleton, Bank of Montreal, Canada's first bank, established the first permanent banking facilities here in 1842.

Then, the bank's agent found himself routinely routed out of bed in the early hours of the morning by lumbermen and trappers who needed cash and an early start.

The hours might be more formal today, but the personal service remains.

Service Specialists

The Bank of Montreal offers a full spectrum of banking services, including trust, investment and lending, through commercial and personal banking specialists. Customer service is offered in-branch, on the telephone or computer, by automated teller or fax machine.

And the bank has taken electronic banking to new frontiers with the launch of mbanx, Canada's first virtual bank. It combines electronic banking with a variety of innovative banking concepts—just one more way that the company keeps pace with changing times.

The rapid technological advances that have made this convenience possible have provided an added bonus for Bank of Montreal's employees and customers. No longer tied to the more routine banking transactions, staff spend more time with customers discussing financial plans.

Specialists, including account managers, investment managers, trust managers and financial services managers, are available to accommodate customers' needs quickly and effectively. The bank's links with other Bank of Montreal companies such as Nesbitt Burns, Harris Bank in Chicago and its alliance with Bancomer, Mexico's largest retail bank ensure seamless extended services for customers, no matter what their needs might be. It's the sort of work that builds customer relationships, much as the community work the bank does builds relationships throughout the region.

Taking the Initiative

The Ottawa-area branches take pride in the number of their staff, at all levels, who are involved with projects as varied as the Children's Aid Society Foundation, the Royal Ottawa Hospital, the Ottawa Heart Institute and the Snowsuit Fund, a worthy program that aims to keep needy children warm in the chilly depths of winter.

The bank actively promotes and supports the efforts of its staff. The Bank of Montreal Group of Companies shares over $17 million a year with charities. This strength in community life comes in part from its network of more than 1,150 locations across the country.

A North American bank with a local focus—as technology continues to advance, so will the bank, always with an eye on the best interests of the customers who come through its doors—real or virtual—every day. ■

The Bank of Montreal offers a full spectrum of banking services, including trust, investment and lending, through commercial and personal banking specialists. Customer service is offered in-branch, on the telephone or computer, by automated teller or fax machine.

Bank of Montreal has been present in Ottawa since 1842. The current Ottawa main branch (left), viewed here from the grounds of Parliament, was opened in 1931. During the opening ceremony, Sir Charles Gordon, then president of Bank of Montreal, said "Our endeavour has been to erect a building which will not only enhance the appearance of the capital, but which will reflect both now and for many years the strength and solidity of the financial structure of our country."

Scott & Aylen

I f you were to drop by the offices of Scott & Aylen as they open in the morning, you'd find staff members pausing in the hallways to exchange greetings and enquire about families. You'd hear the ringing tones of hearty laughter. You'd see people smiling at each other.

They mean it, in every case.

"I came here 18 months ago," says Executive Director Peter Bateman. "Within the first 15 minutes, I felt so very much at home that I knew I'd made the right decision."

The legal and intellectual property firm of Scott & Aylen has an honoured history in Ottawa, but it's focused firmly on the future–of the company itself, and of its clients. Building a team of expert staff, for example, means more to the firm than simply hiring education and experience. It means bringing in people whose skills extend to qualities like trust, mutual respect, creativity and congeniality.

Lawyer Jeremy Farr says that within the resulting collegial atmosphere lies an extremely stable company–experienced and energetic, enthusiastic and forward-thinking.

But staff is only one area in which Scott & Aylen claims ground at the forefront of change. "Law firms historically have provided services on a reactive basis," explains Farr. "But we've adapted to the same sort of business planning cycles as our clients have to follow."

Scott & Aylen has implemented full-time management with non-lawyer executive officers running the firm's operations. And it has developed an organization that has long-term management and growth objectives, in which strategic planning plays an essential part.

One Step Ahead

The family names Scott and Aylen have represented distinguished service in the practice of law for five generations. Colleagues Cuthbert Scott, with expertise in intellectual property, John A. Aylen in litigation, and John G. Aylen in commercial law, formed an association in 1952 which laid the foundations for the current firm.

Today, Scott & Aylen has more than 55 professionals offering fully bilingual legal, patent and trademark services out of offices in Ottawa and Toronto.

Partner David Scott, Cuthbert's son, continues the multi-generational service: the family traces its practice of law to at least 1890 with Sir Richard Scott's law office on Ottawa's Sparks Street. David's emphasis since he joined Scott & Aylen in 1962 has been on its growth.

"We're a traditional law firm that has stayed on the cutting edge because we have emphasized leadership from a dynamic generation," he says. "We're definitely driven to set the standard rather than follow the crowd."

Hence the firm's expansion into commercial law.

Despite its nationally renowned expertise in litigation, Scott & Aylen chose not to rely on this field, but to extend its reach into business law. It was a recognition, in part, that Ottawa's trend was to less dependence on government- and real estate-related law in favour of emerging sectors such as high technology, biotechnology and financial services.

As a result, the 1980s saw Scott & Aylen actively pursuing an expansion of its team: a team that provides a full range of sophisticated services to what

Left to right: Marc Babinski, Bernie Roach, Maureen Clarke, Ed O'Connor, David Scott, Marilyn Prince, Jaspreet Karla, Terrance McManus, Walter Dicesare, Peter Doody, John Aylen, Maria Bossio. Photos by Ari Tapiero.

are now the predominant businesses in the Ottawa marketplace. To achieve this, the firm also drew on its superlative intellectual property background.

"We recognized that we had a unique advantage in our strong, well-known intellectual property practice," says Jeremy Farr. For many of the emerging companies in the high-tech and biotech sectors, intellectual property protection was exactly what they needed to establish themselves. But soon they found they needed specialized commercial services, covering the full range of technology licensing, sales and distribution, securities and financing, employment law and tax planning.

Scott & Aylen was ready for them, offering its full complement of commercial law services on top of the intellectual property capacity for which it was well known. It became "one-stop-shopping" with a twist: each client has one key contact at Scott & Aylen who manages the entire range of needed services with the help of the firm's experts in each area.

This streamlined process can save clients substantial time and legal costs, while ensuring they receive the right advice from the right expert at the right time.

The intellectual property side also anticipated the need for technological expertise, explains Brooke Keneford, patent and trademark agent. "We aggressively expanded our capabilities in the types of technology that will enable us to service these growing sectors," he says. Scott & Aylen hired patent agents with electronics and computer science backgrounds, for instance, to assist high-tech companies.

Marc Jolicoeur, managing partner. Photo by Ari Tapiero.

From patent protection to public share offerings, Scott & Aylen's integrated approach helps its clients generate the business they need, simultaneously maintaining growth and lessening risk.

The Bigger Picture

Marc Jolicoeur, Managing Partner, describes the firm as full service in the realm of what it does best: the three main areas of commercial law, litigation and intellectual property. "Our mission is to serve the best interests of the client," he says simply.

For Scott & Aylen, serving those best interests includes serving a bigger picture—the community at large. "We've always had a lot of involvement in the community and in teaching," says Jolicoeur. The Bar Admission Course, the University of Ottawa, the United Way—each has felt the helping hand of Scott & Aylen's staff.

"We promote and encourage community involvement, both financially and as part of our culture," Jolicoeur explains. "It brings a nice balance to the practice of law. It lets you get a sense first-hand of what the needs of the community are, outside the legal sector, in areas like poverty, education and health."

He summarizes the company's dedication in one motto: If you're going to get involved, get involved to make a difference. The words certainly apply to Scott & Aylen's community work, which traditionally places it well ahead of similar firms in contributions and energy, but they also apply to Scott & Aylen as a legal and intellectual property firm: once again, a step ahead. ■

Hulse, Playfair & McGarry Funeral Homes

The sandstone building at 315 McLeod Street in downtown Ottawa does more than echo the architectural grace of the

The McGarry Family
Erin, Sharon, Brian and Brett

Parliament Buildings: it roots the firm of Hulse, Playfair & McGarry firmly in the soil of the National Capital Region.

The firm has served the nation–from paupers to prime ministers–from the Central Chapel since 1925, providing funeral services and support to thousands of bereaved families.

"It's a trust that's been passed on to us," says Brian McGarry, partner and chief executive officer. He and his wife, Sharon, the firm's president, are majority shareholders, and believe strongly in maintaining local, family control.

The McGarrys have stood by their view despite frequent and substantial offers from other firms. In an industry increasingly marked by large, multinational corporations, Brian and Sharon believe in keeping their destiny in Ottawa.

"We would partner with others across the country, and internationally," says Brian, "but all the time maintaining our local control. Sharon and I believe that we have an institution here in Hulse, Playfair & McGarry . . . and we believe that the trust bestowed on us doesn't include passing the institution on out of local hands."

Brothers Charles and Percy Hulse founded the company in 1925 as Hulse Bros. Funeral Home.

McGarry explains that business in those early days couldn't support two families, so a coin toss determined the brothers' fate. Percy went on to develop a fine funeral home in St. Catharines, Ontario, and Charles stayed in Ottawa.

Keith Playfair joined Charles in the early 1930s, and in 1936 the partners bought their rented McLeod Street building. They added the chapel in 1938, choosing an ecclesiastical design and a stone that would harmonize with the Parliament Buildings.

Brian McGarry arrived in 1962 at the age of 17, working with both Hulse and Playfair. The McGarry Family began buying into the company in 1972, acquiring a majority share in 1987. It was a busy year. The historic Central Chapel was expanded and refurbished, while the company itself formed a relationship with Trillium Funeral Service, a group of Canadian funeral homes that today has a 45 per cent share in Hulse, Playfair & McGarry. The affiliation brought new strengths to the firm, while maintaining its local character and ownership.

Hulse, Playfair & McGarry is today one of the largest family-controlled businesses in Canada, with four funeral home locations in the Ottawa-Carleton region and a fifth being built in Quebec's Chelsea-Wakefield area, from which the McGarrys originally hail.

In all of these locations, the compassionate care offered to clientele and the firm's attention to society's changing needs have helped the number of funerals a year grow from 900 in 1987 to more than 1,600 a decade later.

McGarry explains that funeral services have moved toward providing an experience to the bereaved family, and have expanded in scope to match society's diversity.

Hulse, Playfair & McGarry takes a unique satisfaction in serving the community's total spectrum. From state funerals for such dignitaries as former prime ministers John Diefenbaker and Lester B. Pearson, to simpler, family-oriented ceremonies to no-frills memorial services, the firm aims to fulfil every family's wishes.

This has led to such community-oriented projects as Ottawa's first Reception Centre. Located across from the Central Chapel, the Centre offers a friendly, relaxed atmosphere for those wishing to hold receptions after funeral services. "Moving from the formality of the funeral home to the informality of the Reception Centre provides a psychological break for families," says Brian. The idea proved so well received that all Hulse, Playfair & McGarry locations now offer "After Funeral Care."

Located with the Reception Centre is the Resource Centre, an extensive resource library dealing with all aspects of death, dying and grieving. The Centre is open to any member of the public seeking information, and to those studying bereavement.

Hulse, Playfair & McGarry also developed its own booklet on bereavement, *A Guide to Understanding Grief,* which is used by local palliative care centres and distributed free to the public. *Frontline,* a quarterly newsletter, is dedicated to professional and volunteer care-givers. The firm makes much of this information available over the Internet as well, through its Web site. Staff also have excellent links to outside resource people to whom they can refer those in need.

The firm's personal touch is evident throughout its operations. No answering machines are used; staff are on duty 24 hours a day to ensure that the public always has access to someone experienced in funeral service.

While the company can accommodate a full range of requests, the McGarry Family has developed a special option for those wishing simplified funeral services. Their nationally registered Simplicity Plan®–based on philosophy as much as finances–is currently offered out of the Memorial Funeral Home on Somerset Street West and will soon be available at the Memorial Chapel and Crematorium in the Outaouais.

Through the company and their personal lives, Brian and Sharon are tireless in their pursuit of a better community for all, serving such groups as Kiwanis, Action Paramedic and Bereaved Families of Ontario. Brian co-founded Dialogue Canada in the Ottawa area, a non-profit, non-

The Central Chapel: "Serving the nation from paupers to prime ministers since 1925."

partisan, non-governmental citizens' group dedicated to encouraging communication among society's diverse elements, and a strong advocate of Canadian unity.

Sharon is particularly proud of the company's contribution to the making of a Camp Trillium video; the Ontario summer camp hosts children who have cancer.

A highlight of community life for the McGarrys is the Ottawa Senators National Hockey League team. Brian and Sharon are among a group of Ottawa families who originally invested in the team, and Brian has fond memories of the day the NHL announced the franchise's awarding to Ottawa: he and his son were on hand for the announcement in Florida.

Although having served local politics as an education trustee and regional councillor, Brian McGarry remains staunchly non-partisan, preferring to put the business first.

As Hulse, Playfair & McGarry looks to the future, the firm's founding creed echoes through the years, and through its dedication to the citizens in the National Capital Region. "To alleviate the sorrow of parting is to render a service to community. To this, our every effort is respectfully dedicated." ■

Modest beginnings: the original funeral home and hearse for Hulse Bros.

Blake, Cassels & Graydon

*B*lake, Cassels & Graydon offers its clients the best of all possible worlds: full-service corporate legal work, backed by the strength and resources of a national firm and provided through their well-known office at the very centre of Ottawa.

Left to right: Gord Cameron, Matthew Halpin, Don Greenfield, Eric Elvidge.

"Blakes in Ottawa has all the advantages of a small office," says administrative partner Matt Halpin. "We can give our clients the personal, intimate support that helps them establish a long-term relationship with us."

A strong local profile, together with access to the expertise and experience of more than 350 lawyers in offices across Canada, gives Blakes a unique position from which to serve its clients.

At the same time, the Ottawa lawyers of Blakes have access to extensive services—including one of the largest private law libraries in Canada—that

help them deal with the sophisticated, challenging legal work found in Ottawa-Carleton's vibrant business and high-tech community.

Through a formal association with a Quebec-based firm and its bilingual Ottawa office, Blakes also serves businesses in the Outaouais area. The firm's affiliation with Lex Mundi, an international legal referral and information exchange service, allows Blakes to handle the worldwide needs of its Ottawa clients, as well as assist clients from around the world with Ottawa-based interests.

A listing with Lex Mundi demonstrates a certain standing in the legal community. In the case of Blakes, it reflects the firm's position as one of the oldest and largest law firms in Canada. Established in 1856 in Toronto, Blakes has been involved in many of the significant legal and business developments in Canadian history: founder Edward Blake himself did the legal work to set up what is now the Canadian Imperial Bank of Commerce.

Blakes' Ottawa office opened in 1990 and is now well established. Eric Elvidge, a Blakes partner who practises securities law, explains: "We have a very strong group here in Ottawa. We also benefit from all the resources of a large, long-established national law firm with excellent international connections. This gives us a tremendous advantage."

This easily enables the office to assist local high-tech companies as they develop from private into public entities. "In fact, much of our corporate securities work is based on the high-tech sector," notes Blakes lawyer Gary Jessop.

Blakes is very familiar with the particular needs of high-tech operations: the firm has acted on most of Ottawa's recent initial public offerings, and has assisted a number of local companies as they progressed from small, high-growth organizations, through their debut onto the public stage, to the point where they are now large Ottawa-based companies with a strong international presence.

The firm's pragmatic, constructive and result-oriented attitude provides solutions for its clients rather than problems. Blakes aims to provide clear and practical advice, assisting its clients to achieve their objectives in a sensible and cost-effective manner.

Through its progressive approach, Blakes not only works with leading-edge companies, but is on the forefront of development in Canadian legal matters. The firm uses the latest computer technology in its ongoing efforts to extend the benefit of its integrated national databases of legal precedents, memoranda and opinions to all its lawyers, and to serve its clients for the lowest possible cost. This allows Blakes to avoid "reinventing the wheel" wherever possible.

A thorough professional training program led by a full-time director of continuing legal education assists Blakes lawyers to develop and refine their skills throughout their careers.

As a full-service firm, Blakes includes the following among its areas of expertise: administrative; banking and financial institutions; broadcasting; charitable organizations; civil litigation; competition and antitrust; corporate and commercial; employment and labour; pensions and benefits; environmental; estates and trust; high-tech financing; insolvency; intellectual property; international trade; real estate; mergers and acquisitions; municipal; publishing and communications; taxation; telecommunications; oil and gas; and securities.

Creative thinking, focused on the client, embodies the Blakes approach to law. To alert clients to emerging issues that may affect them, the firm issues various newsletters and specialized publications directed at particular segments of its clientele. It also hosts educational seminars. The firm is also assisting the Ontario Securities Commission to rewrite its policies and formulate new new rules. In this way, the firm uses its collective knowledge and experience to anticipate developments, identify opportunities and bring to its clients new perspectives and ideas.

Keeping in touch with its clients includes the wider community. Blakes encourages its staff to pursue outside activities and interests, which in Ottawa include the Children's Aid Society and the United Way. The balance created between work and other interests helps the firm's lawyers maintain their fresh outlook.

Matthew Halpin is looking forward to the future in Ottawa. "We expect to continue growing and prospering with the city," he says of Blakes. "The opportunities for exciting legal work, plus the green spaces and accessibility of the Ottawa area, make it a great community in which to live and work."

As Blake, Cassels & Graydon approaches a century and a half of practice in Canada, it can look with pride at the business law innovations it has produced and to the future with a continuing enthusiasm and commitment to its clients. ∎

Seated, left to right: Bruce Caughill, Hugh Hospodar, Kathy Podrebarac. Standing, left to right: John Lawrence, Debra Armstrong, Gary Jessop, Nancy Brooks.

John Lawrence

E.B. Eddy Forest Products Ltd.

When Ezra Butler Eddy and his wife arrived in Hull, Quebec, in search of new ventures in 1851, he began a small match manufacturing enterprise, producing 10 cases of matches daily.

Today, the companies within the E.B. Eddy group form an integrated forest products entity with large forest management areas, four sawmills and a pulp and paper mill in northern Ontario and paper mills in Canada and the U.S.–and they haven't manufactured a match since 1928.

By 1857, E.B. Eddy had added several new lines of wooden products, including washboards, pails and clothes pins, and in the early 1860s he installed several generators on the Chaudière Falls along the Ottawa River in order to power his growing enterprises.

It was in 1866 when he began his foray into the lumber business, with the renting of a small sawmill. Realizing its potential, he purchased property and built his own sawmill in 1870 beside the Ottawa River near his match factory. He then purchased timber rights to the north to provide the raw material that would eventually help his sawmill become one of the largest in the world.

By 1880, with several more sawmills, the company was turning out 75 million feet of lumber a year and 185 cases of matches a day, in addition to the products that the planing mill, sash and door factory and box factory were producing. Ezra consolidated his various companies into The E.B. Eddy Company in 1886, added a chemical pulp factory in 1889, and the following year installed the company's first paper machine.

The E.B. Eddy Company in 1901 had seven paper machines in operation producing 80 tons a day of various papers, including ledger, writing, litho, book, news, poster, drug, tea, cover, manilla, brown wrapping, tissue, cardboard and wood pulp board.

The scope of the company's operations continued after E.B. Eddy passed away in 1906. Garfield Weston purchased a controlling interest in 1943, and The E.B. Eddy Company eventually became a division of George Weston Limited, a position which it still enjoys today.

For decades, E.B. Eddy's Ottawa-Hull mills produced tissue papers and a range of lightweight papers used in the printing of bibles and encyclopedias. In fact, for many years, E.B. Eddy was the largest producer of bible paper in North America. In the mid-80s, the company decided to focus its operations on value-added markets and subsequently sold the Hull tissue mill.

Adding value is an important aspect of E.B. Eddy's operations. The company has established a track record for specialized products and excellent service in papermaking. In 1994, the No. 14 paper machine at Ottawa-Hull was rebuilt in order to develop a new range of lightweight coated grades targeted for the commercial printing and book publishing markets. These new grades are marketed under the names Lighthouse Matte, Spinnaker Matte, Ocean Cote and Schooner Matte and Gloss.

Today, E.B. Eddy is well-known as a leading manufacturer of coated and uncoated fine, specialty and packaging grade papers, including recycled content paper grades. In addition to its paper mills in Ottawa-Hull and Espanola, the company has, over the past decade, acquired paper mills in Port Huron, Michigan and Delta, British Columbia.

Specialty papers involve working in close partnership with customers to develop products to fit specific applications. Years of papermaking experience, through the skills and dedication of the company's papermakers, have produced specialty papers designed for an array of end uses, including backing for sandpaper, special release paper for self-adhesive products, transfer paper for printing processes, sterilizable paper for packaging medical products and even the unique paper produced for the manufacture of surgical garments.

In 1995, E.B. Eddy introduced a new coated paper grade called Bravo through its Delta, B.C., Division-Island Paper Mills, with high brightness and high gloss characteristics. Island Paper Mills is one of a select group of North American opera-

Ezra Butler Eddy - 1828 to 1906

tions manufacturing the highest quality coated paper products.

Paper recycling is part of the E.B. Eddy commitment to caring for the environment. Several of E.B. Eddy's paper products contain a minimum of 50 per cent recycled content with 20 per cent of the recycled being post-consumer. Eddy's Guardian Opaque and matching cover are both certified by the Canadian Environmental Choice Program carrying the coveted EcoLogo and exceed current EPA guidelines.

Supporting the papermaking capabilities of E.B. Eddy are its pulp, forestry and wood products divisions.

For the 4.6 million hectares of forest land in northern Ontario under either direct or indirect management by E.B. Eddy, the company prepares 20-year management plans which include planning for harvesting, forest regeneration and environmental protection. The company plants and seeds millions of trees every year and believes that its forest management practices are sustainable. The company has committed to the registration of its directly managed forest lands under recognized programs such as the Canadian Standards Association's (CSA) Sustainable Forest Management Standard.

E.B. Eddy's sawmills at Nairn Centre (Ontario's largest sawmill), Elk Lake, Timmins and Sault Ste. Marie have an annual output of about 395 million board feet, and produce softwood and hardwood lumber, hardwood veneer, residual chips and pulpwood. Close proximity to market and exacting standards ensure a quality product, whether it be lumber for home and building construction, specialty wood for the framing and furniture industry or hardwood veneers. Sawmill personnel strive for maximum lumber yield, using every part of the tree: bark and sawdust fuel the kilns, while chips go to the company's pulp mill.

At its Espanola pulp mill, E.B. Eddy was the first company in North America to use the oxygen delignification process prior to bleaching, resulting in 50 per cent less chlorine in the first bleaching stage, a significant environmental improvement. The resulting top-grade pulp feeds the company's paper operations, as well as those of its customers. By 1999, E.B. Eddy will have installed ozone bleaching technology, another Canadian first for the company to ensure continuous improvement in process and product quality and environmental protection.

Sustainable forest management is crucial to the long-term success of E.B. Eddy.

E.B. Eddy Forest Products Ltd. has shown itself to be a leader. To achieve this leadership position, the company has invested its time, money and experience in product improvement and environmental protection, and enhancing its services to meet the needs of a changing world. Through its people, with their strong sense of pride in their work, and through application of the latest technology, E.B. Eddy will continue to be at the forefront of new ideas, with a philosophy developed by its founder that has truly stood the test of time. ∎

Modern technology and a well-trained workforce are key to producing a quality product.

Otto & Erskine Architects Inc.

"*A*sset management."
"Building envelope design."
"Forensic architecture."

These terms might not automatically come to mind when one thinks "architecture," but for Otto & Erskine Architects Inc., they're integral to the firm's approach.

Herbert Otto founded the practice in 1979. It became Otto & Erskine in January 1996, when Otto and Gordon Erskine, long-time colleagues, joined forces as partners. The partners' combined experience covers new building design, retrofitting and renovation projects for a variety of clients, including private homeowners, housing cooperatives, institutional and government buildings as well as private businesses. Their current services encompass a building's total life cycle, featuring design, maintenance planning, troubleshooting and retrofit.

Particular pride is reserved for the solutions offered clients faced with existing building stock requiring maintenance or upgrading. Using a crossover between engineering and architecture, the firm's forensic architecture skills pinpoint sources of trouble and provide customized solutions. Troubleshooting offers its own rewards. Remedial work on current buildings, when incorporated into new building designs or retrofits, adds outstanding value to a building's life cycle. Backed with a thorough understanding of building science, it enables the firm to make design decisions with the client's bottom line in mind—for both current and long-term costs. Communication and value form Otto & Erskine's foundations: the firm places a strong emphasis on its service-oriented attitude. It listens to clients, to their needs and limitations, and it meets those needs with well-built, functional building projects that arrive on time and on budget.

Of course, functional projects don't preclude imagination and innovation. Design work on Ottawa's Lady Evelyn Alternative School

Otto Bryden Erskine Martel Architects Incorporated

Lady Evelyn Alternative School

garnered an Award of Merit from the Ontario Association of Architects. Planned through a unique consultation between the architects, school board,

Otto Bryden Erskine Martel Architects Incorporated

Two Auriga Drive

teachers and parents, the school facility now operates to rave reviews.

The firm's range is also demonstrated with the OHSC Co-generation Facility, a $70-million generating plant at the Ottawa Health Sciences Centre. Designed, built and placed into operation within two years, the building produces steam, hot water and electricity for five hospitals, and sells power to Ontario Hydro. The firm handled the building design and the approval processes within the hospitals and among the four levels of government involved.

Otto & Erskine serves Eastern Ontario— from Kingston to Pembroke, and Hawkesbury to Cornwall, with a strong presence in Ottawa-Carleton. The firm's work further afield, in Germany for Canada Mortgage and Housing Corporation, adds another dimension to its portfolio.

This expertise is proving useful as the firm participates in Canada's National Task Force to develop a new, objective-based national building code for the 21st century. But perhaps the best example of Otto & Erskine's work is its own offices, in the bright, spacious loft of an old church hall. An excellent adaptive re-use project for which the firm acted as both architects and general contractors, it offers a reference few could argue with. ∎

Finlayson & Singlehurst

With clients ranging from corporate attorneys to advanced technology manufacturers, Finlayson & Singlehurst is a small law firm that specializes in patent, trade mark, copyright and industrial design law, known generally as "intellectual property" law. Backed by a 30-year track record of efficient, personalized service by its members, the firm is well known for its professional expertise. The firm is licensed to practice before the Canadian Intellectual Property Office, and its members are all registered patent and trade-mark agents as well as lawyers.

"Essentially our practice concentrates on agency and associate work for foreign corporations and attorneys representing clients seeking to secure and protect intellectual property rights in Canada," explains John Singlehurst, who has been in the business since 1969. "As a relatively small firm, we believe we can and do offer quality service at an economical price."

John Singlehurst, whose professional expertise spans both mechanical engineering and intellectual property law, was a patent examiner with the Canadian Patent Office (now the Canadian Intellectual Property Office) before joining Don Finlayson in practice in 1969.

Donald Finlayson, with a background in mining engineering, has recently retired but continues to act as an advisor to the practice on a daily basis.

Hugh Campbell is a specialist in electrical products, systems and design, particularly when applied to communications and computer technology. Hugh originally began working with Don and John as a law student in 1977, having an electrical engineering background. Hugh rejoined Don and John in the practice after spending three years in London, England, with a leading intellectual property litigation firm and several years in Canada with another firm.

When Don Finlayson and John Singlehurst entered into practice, the location of the firm in the National Capital Region provided an advantage because of its proximity to the government patent and copyright office in Ottawa-Hull. In more recent years, electronic communication has rendered location less important than it once was, but it can nevertheless still prove to be an advantage at times from a cost point of view, particularly for those cases requiring personal intervention. The partnership enjoys an international reputation built on long experience with Canadian intellec-

tual property practice and related cases.

The vast majority of Finlayson & Singlehurst's clients are from the United States, Europe and Japan. The firm has sought Canadian patents, industrial designs and trade marks on behalf of major corporations across industry, including major manufacturers of personal computers, photography, mail sorting products, clothes and dishwashing machines, electrical hardware components and batteries, as well as for the technology research branches of major foreign governments and numerous foreign universities. Although the firm has concentrations in mechanical and electrical patents, its clients represent a broad cross-section of industrial research sectors, including entities and universities doing chemical and medical research.

The occasional offbeat inventions come through the office, Campbell says. Every patent agent seems to patent a gadget to keep toilet seats from being left up, and he is no exception. "But most of the things that we see are a little more sophisticated," he reflects. A typical list ranges from the low-tech to the very high-tech: from board games, toys and fishing lures through processes for making glass, braking systems for vehicles, industrial furnaces, laser measuring devices, medical and surgical equipment, manufacturing methods and composition of synthetic fibres, to digital telephony apparatus, new forms of electronic semi-conductors, personal computers and a wide variety of other computer-related patents touching upon virtually every field in the industry. ■

John Singlehurst and Hugh Campbell

"The Firm" (seated, left to right)
Don Finlayson, Hugh Campbell
(standing, left to right) Diane
McKeen, Nicole Richer, Sharon
Ambridge, Wendy Hanna,
John Singlehurst, Karen Page,
Joan Lothian

179

Continental Mushroom Corporation Ltd.

Grower of some of the finest mushrooms in the world, Continental Mushroom Corp. is among the largest mushroom farms in Ontario. Located in Metcalfe, Ontario, just outside Ottawa, Continental Mushroom has successfully blended a unique farming style,

In 1990 Continental Mushroom was chosen one of Canada's top 50 privately owned businesses.

ingenious engineering techniques and a dedicated labour force, with a family atmosphere that permeates its stadium-size buildings. The result is an expanding business that supplies fresh mushrooms across Canada and into the United States.

Continental's story begins after World War II with Nicholas Pora, a refugee from Romania with a background in industrial chemistry. Nick Senior, as he is known today, immigrated to Canada in 1950 and found a job on a small Ontario mushroom farm. This was his introduction to a changing industry where a good education and a

Nicholas Pora, founder of Continental Mushroom Corporation Ltd.

sharp mind were rapidly replacing a strong back as a requirement for success, Pora recalls.

After working as a manager for growers in Quebec and Ontario, Pora established his own mushroom farm at Metcalfe in 1972. Beginning with a 138,000-square-foot area, he had to recruit and teach his workers the basics of the business, from operating the crane trucks to harvesting, packing and marketing the mushrooms.

By 1980, the farm's growing surface was more than double the original, and a few years later Pora added an office building with packing, cooling and shipping facilities. In 1985, the company opened a distribution centre in Montreal.

Innovation is a way of life at Continental, starting with the unconventional style of mushroom-growing beds pioneered by Pora when he began the farm. To maximize production and minimize costs, Continental's mushroom beds are stacked 12 high rather than the typical 6 layers. The result is a "high" style of beds topping out at over 20 feet and divided into 3 storeys. This configuration has required Pora and company engineers to use their ingenuity in adapting machinery and custom designing production techniques over time.

As well, Continental uses new technology, such as computer-controlled systems that regulate temperature and humidity, to continually increase production. The company harvests more than 12 tons of mushrooms a day in its 33 growing houses.

Every day, some 250 workers are transported to Continental from the surrounding communities of Ottawa, Hull and Gatineau on the company's "mushroom" buses, which are also often loaned to local nursery schools for field trips. Because many are recent immigrants, Continental invited a local school board to initiate a special educational program on the farm. The board developed a unique "literacy in the workplace" pilot project, and an on-site classroom was built. Now workers may take both group and individual lessons, and the program also offers instruction leading to Canadian citizenship.

Over the years, Continental Mushroom has evolved into an extended family business, with Pora's wife, son, two daughters and a son-in-law working with the company. At the same time, Continental has achieved management excellence; in 1990 the company was chosen one of Canada's top 50 privately owned businesses. ∎

CHAPTER FOURTEEN

Health Care, Education & the Public Sector

Courtesy University of Ottawa

World Heart Corporation

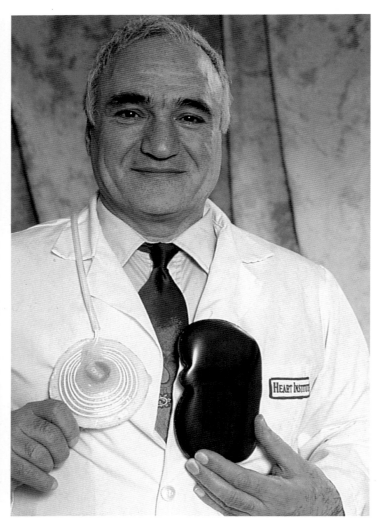

Dr. Tofy Mussivand, HeartSaver VAD developer and WorldHeart president, demonstrates the size and placement of the HeartSaver VAD system.

*H*eart failure kills more than 5 million people worldwide every year, including some 45,000 Canadians and 500,000 Americans. Thanks, however, to a young, start-up company located in Ottawa and backed by the area's leading entrepreneurs and researchers, hope for an effective, long-term treatment for this debilitating condition lies around the corner of the 21st century.

World Heart Corporation, or WorldHeart, was formed in April 1996 to bring the Ottawa Heart Institute's work from the laboratory bench to the general public. In its initial public offering in December 1996, the firm issued 35 per cent of its shares to the public and raised approximately $17 million to help fuel development work.

The company's focus is the HeartSaver VAD (ventricular assist device), a small, lightweight artificial heart which can assist or replace the natural heart's pumping action. The HeartSaver VAD, fully implantable and capable of remote power, monitor and control, has the potential to revolutionize the treatment of heart failure—and save millions of lives.

Cardiovascular disease in general is the leading cause of death in Canada, the United States and most of the developed world, where it accounts for 40 to 50 per cent of all deaths. Heart failure causes approximately half of those deaths, marked by the heart muscle's progressive deterioration and a decreasing ability to pump sufficient blood around the body.

It's a slow and painful disease, almost always fatal, which often strikes at an early age. An estimated 40 per cent of those suffering from heart failure are under 65 and in their prime productive years. Its toll in terms of lengthy, expensive medical treatment, lost wages and decreased productivity is priceless—but rising as the disease's prevalence increases.

Current treatment methods for heart failure have significant limitations. Medication, often the first line of defence, offers only symptomatic relief, slowing but not preventing the disease's progression. Heart transplantation is an effective but limited option due to the lack of available donor organs (currently less than 3,000 worldwide per year) and medication to prevent the body's immune system from rejecting the donor heart makes patients vulnerable to other disease.

Although the medical community continues to research other options, it is the artificial heart which holds out the greatest hope.

Now in use within hospitals as "bridges" until heart transplant surgery can occur, artificial hearts have already saved thousands of lives. They come in two forms: total artificial hearts (TAHs), which completely replace the natural heart, and VADs, which assist or maintain the heart's pumping action without actually replacing the heart.

Because TAHs involve such issues as the loss of the natural heart's neurological control mechanisms, the artificial heart of choice is the VAD.

Its advantages are clear: an endless supply, available on an emergency basis, no blood type matching issues, no need for immunosuppressant drugs, immediate improvement in blood circulation after implant, the potential for natural heart recovery, and an expected improvement in the user's quality of life due to the lack of continuing medication.

The VADs currently on the market are limited to in-hospital bridge use, in part because they require the use of wires and tubes to connect the device with exterior controls and monitors. These external connections also significantly increase the risk of infection. The HeartSaver VAD System, however, uses a transcutaneous energy transfer (TET) system to move electrical energy through the patient's intact skin and tissue to either charge the VAD's internal battery or directly power it. The biotelemetry system, meanwhile, uses infrared and radio transmitter/receiver modules embedded in the TET system to transmit information back and forth.

The HeartSaver VAD system has other advantages over present technology. Its design allows implantation in the chest cavity next to the heart, a far less invasive surgery than current abdomen implantation and a simpler, more reliable connection system to the natural heart. Smaller and lighter than existing VADs, it can be used for assisting the heart's left or right ventricle, or even both. The lack of wires and tubes allows patients to regain normal, everyday living routines.

In addition, the system has the potential for substantial health care system cost savings, due to decreased reliance on continuing medication, and the HeartSaver's totally implantable nature. The HeartSaver VAD is expected to undergo clinical trials in 1999 and reach general availability in 2001.

The HeartSaver VAD was developed at the Cardiovascular Devices Division (CVD) of the Ottawa Heart Institute Research Corporation (OHIRC), a non-profit research affiliate of the University of Ottawa Heart Institute, which itself was founded under the leadership of Dr. Wilbert Keon in 1976 as a joint undertaking of the University of Ottawa and the Ottawa Civic Hospital.

The HeartSaver VAD Program was established in 1988, with research conducted under the direction of Dr. Tofy Mussivand, who now serves as WorldHeart's president and chief operating officer in addition to his duties as CVD's director and principal investigator. Funded primarily by contributions from the Canadian and Ontario governments and private donations, CVD developed a technically advanced working prototype of the HeartSaver VAD system in preparation for testing in animals. Earlier prototypes of the VAD have performed failure-free for more than four years on the bench.

Taking the system to the general public would require even more substantial funding, however, and the Heart Institute turned to Rod Bryden, already well known in Ottawa for co-founding high-tech giant SHL Systemhouse and for helping to bring the Ottawa Senators NHL team back to Ottawa fans. Impressed with the Institute's progress and its project management record, Bryden teamed with the Heart Institute, Corel Chairman Michael Cowpland and Dr. Tofy Mussivand to form World Heart Corporation in April 1996.

Dr. Cowpland provided advice to CVD on state-of-the-art software for the HeartSaver VAD during the early design process. When WorldHeart was formed, Dr. Cowpland was a founder and serves on WorldHeart's board of directors. His experience in founding Corel in Ottawa, and taking it worldwide in a sector marked by stiff international competition, is a tremendous asset to WorldHeart.

The Ottawa Heart Institute, under the leadership of Dr. Wilbert Keon, brings a depth of expertise and experience recognized around the world. The Institute offers specialized cardiac care in a 118-bed facility located adjacent to the Ottawa Civic Hospital, and is internationally recognized for cardiac care and the pre-clinical and clinical evaluation of cardiovascular devices. Dr. Keon chairs the WorldHeart Clinical Advisory Board of eminent professionals.

WorldHeart brings together a team that combines business acumen with leading-edge research and development resources and clinical expertise—a uniquely Ottawa team that is bringing the region worldwide attention as the home of the next crucial development in heart failure treatment. ■

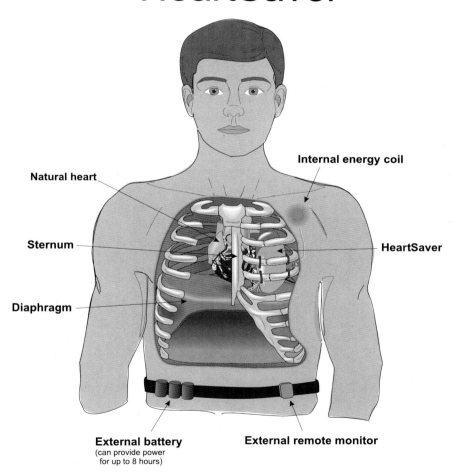

HeartSaver

WorldHeart is focused on the HeartSaver VAD, a small, lightweight artificial heart that holds out the strongest treatment hope for the millions of people worldwide who suffer the debilitating effects of heart failure.

Ottawa Catholic Schools

School Year 1996-97 marks 140 years of service by Ottawa Catholic Schools to the Catholic community—young people and adults—residing in Ottawa, Vanier and Rockcliffe Park.

"Right now, education is the most important function in my life. Being in a Catholic school just makes my education even more valuable. It enables me to incorporate my religious faith into my education. With the belief in God at the centre of my education, I feel that I am never alone in my journey to achieve success."

– Fern Banatyne, OAC

Schools: Fully Alive

Since 1856, more than 10 years before Confederation, Ottawa Catholic Schools have offered "Education Plus," education that is concerned with the spirit, the intellect, the physical, the social and the emotional—thus with the whole child. Truly education that is fully alive!

Visit one of its 33 facilities. This concept has stood the test of time. The Ottawa Roman Catholic Separate School Board, in partnership, pursues its mission to provide quality education, guidance and support to its students, nurturing their spiritual growth and challenging them to be fully alive.

There is a place for everyone. Educators, academic and administrative staff, parents, clergy, volunteers and the students themselves are dedicated to meeting the challenges of each child and adult student.

The Ottawa Roman Catholic Separate School Board serves over 11,000 students representing a diverse population of Canadians, as well as recent immigrants from nearly 100 countries around the world. These students share the marvellous flavour of ethnic communities, while city neighbourhoods offer wonderful, long-standing traditions. In this lively atmosphere, the schools ensure equity of opportunity for all students.

Education is . . .
". . . doing your pluses."

– Ramon Monsour, Grade 1

". . . playing nice."

– Jordan Hamilton, Grade 1

Sound Fundamentals

Ottawa Catholic Schools focus on good, solid essential educational programming—in reading, writing and computing—within the context of faith development. Each school offers similar Ontario-based courses, with expertise from educational professionals infused with Gospel values.

Kindergarten classrooms are bright, active places. Teachers and programs stimulate each child's creativity and curiosity. French Immersion from senior kindergarten to grade six and core French in later grades assist those who wish to become bilingual and offer others vitally important linguistic formation.

Technology is a key focus. The arts, humanities, sciences and maths are also strongly featured in courses established to challenge intermediate and senior students alike. Throughout the schools, computer-enriched learning with Internet access enhances education.

Ottawa's Catholic Schools serve exceptional students—those who experience special challenges with learning—with a range of programs and services. Those who are gifted and those who require developmental support can find a home in the schools. Services for new Canadians include English as a Second Language (ESL), while summer school programs help students develop better mathematics and language skills. Students learn about and practise peer mediation and peacemaking to resolve conflict.

Extracurricular activities and special programs enliven the school year. Budding scientists participate in science fairs, mathematics Olympics or even simulated missions to Mars. The artistically inclined express their interests through drama clubs, bands, choirs, arts programs or school papers and yearbooks. The athletic find plenty of opportunities with numerous programs and strong teams in every appropriate sport.

And for those interested in issues, clubs available are public speaking, multicultural, social justice and environment. Through every grade, students learn about fair play, gain leadership skills, make new friends and witness the example of fine educators.

Ottawa Catholic Schools offer students opportunities to participate in the real world of work through a host of cooperative education programs. Partnerships with numerous businesses allow the schools to draw on enriched expertise, technological support, leadership and, indeed, mentorship from the local community. Business thereby enhances the skills of future employees and learns from educators about services to people.

Meanwhile, the three Schools of Community Education, in community partnership, serve an annual enrollment of over 15,000 learners of all ages in programs that include ESL, international languages, citizenship and numeracy.

Education . . .

". . . prepares me for the rest of my life, not only a career."

– Anika Clarke, Grade 12

Sharing the Strengths of the Community

Partnerships—with parents and parent committees, with parishes and with the broader community—form a cornerstone of Ottawa Catholic Schools' approach to education. School advisory councils have formalized these relationships.

Volunteers, including retirees and seniors, business people, university and college students, scientists and service club members, play a key role in the success of many programs, becoming true partners in the learning process. Various homework clubs and tutoring and mentoring programs rely heavily on volunteers to provide friendly support and positive role models, while easing school career concerns.

Businesses in the community, through donations of resources or employee time, make many special programs possible, while schools welcome individuals with specialized knowledge or experiences who share their skills with students.

Partnerships with parishes are integral to the development and learning that take place. Religious instruction and the living example of Catholic educators are key elements of the schools' strategies to bring faith development programs to the students. Thus, Catholicism infuses all areas of study and school life.

One special partnership worth noting is with other school boards. Area taxpayers save millions

each year through cooperative provision of special education programs, joint purchasing and school buses . . . to name but a few.

These partnerships, and the focus on providing an environment that lets each child become fully alive, have resulted in schools that are full of life and the spirit of the Gospel. The nature of education has changed since Ottawa Catholic Schools began, but its motto still holds true in the corridors of its schools and the hearts of its students: *"Age Quod Agis*–What you do, do well."

"Education unveils the richness and goodness that is in man and imparts the knowledge of what we should each be striving for: the improvement of our future and the world."

– Ben Librande, Grade 12

140 Years of Service

The year 1998 ushers in a new era. Ottawa Catholic Schools will amalgamate with Carleton Catholic Schools. The new Ottawa-Carleton District Catholic School Board will bear the hallmarks of the best of both systems . . . and so the tradition will continue! ■

Algonquin College of Applied Arts and Technology

Technology that increases in power and complexity, seemingly overnight . . . restructuring that fundamentally changes that which an organization expects of its employees . . . a world in which lightning-fast communication creates opportunity, and competition . . . .

In a fast-paced, constantly changing environment, an organization relies on one resource to anticipate those changes and overcome the challenges: the skills of its people. For over 30 years, Algonquin College has provided corporate and government sectors with highly skilled people who bring valuable assets like vision, flexibility and practical training to their employment.

Founded in 1967 to provide an alternative form of post-secondary education, Algonquin today is a global provider of training and education, with a strong mandate in retraining and skills upgrading to meet the challenges of today's workplace.

Algonquin delivers more than 130 government-accredited programs and 2,500 individual courses through its Schools of Business and Applied Arts, Health Sciences, Technology and Trades and Continuing Education. Its curriculum, taught by 524 full-time professors and 2,500 part-time instructors, serves more than 70,000 people annually on a variety of major campuses in the Ottawa Valley.

Students enjoy skill-based, applied training in a practical environment: Algonquin has invested millions to provide the facilities and technology required by organizations operating in highly competitive, rapidly advancing, technology-based fields.

The focal point of Algonquin College of Applied Arts and Technology, the main campus in Ottawa is one of several major Algonquin campuses in the Ottawa Valley.

Algonquin College offers its students a complete college experience, including an extensive array of student services, an active campus life, and world-class instruction.

Customized Corporate Training—Delivering Solutions That Fit

Algonquin's corporate training services reflect the College's commitment to be at the forefront of technological revolution, providing leading-edge training and education to the corporate sector and various levels of government.

More than 500 organizations—local, national and international—annually take advantage of Algonquin's customized training solutions to help them keep pace with technological change, improve managerial and entrepreneurial skills and enhance productivity.

Algonquin's goal is straightforward: to help its business clients improve their performance, but its approach sets it apart. The College takes the time to listen to the unique needs of each client, and develops solutions that respond specifically to those needs.

Training solutions are practical and immediately transferable to the workplace with highly flexible delivery options. Clients may choose Algonquin's central, well-equipped facilities or their own locations, and may choose the time and method of delivery that best suits their schedule. Algonquin's superior technical support and extensive distance education experience enable the College to offer training in person, or through innovative distance options—including online.

This flexibility comes from Algonquin's solid understanding of the employers and students it serves. The College's faculty members are industry-trained, having worked in their chosen fields for many years. They stay current with industry practices and developments, always in touch with the challenges inherent in the real world.

Through more than 100 advisory committees, the College forges dynamic and continuing links with industry, corporate and government sectors. This ensures that students receive training appropriate to industry requirements, while providing employers with an exceptional labour pool.

In addition, Algonquin constantly pursues and obtains business and industry partnerships that foster mutual growth and innovation. These strategic partnerships, with such giants as SHL Systemhouse, Silicon Graphics and Digital Equipment, hold key benefits for both partners. Digital, for example, has its parts tested at Algonquin, providing students with outstanding experience, and the company with graduates already trained in Digital products.

The International Education Centre–Answering Global Challenges

With its International Education Centre, Algonquin has extended its expertise in technical, vocational and business training to include the world. It welcomes international students to the College and responds to training requests worldwide.

The Centre offers international project management expertise and a portfolio of training products with wide-ranging content: from human resource development and institutional management to strategic planning and financial management; curriculum development and teacher training to public relations and information technology. Designing and delivering management training for the governments of such countries as Egypt, Jordan, Botswana and Hungary has given the Centre a rich background of experience from which to draw.

While the Centre has delivered training assistance to 35 countries around the world, students from more than 50 countries have chosen to study at Algonquin. These students not only put their newly acquired knowledge and skills to use in their home countries, but often Canadian technologies as well.

Centres of Excellence–The Heart of Algonquin

For students, international governments and corporate clients alike, Algonquin's Centres of Excellence provide trusted leadership.

The Media Centre, for example, is a state-of-the-art, 50,000-square-foot facility that has made Algonquin College a leader in new media and non-linear technology. With advanced industry-standard training in interactive multimedia, digital animation, electronic audio-video editing and electronic publishing, the Centre serves the growing high-technology industry, already attracting an impressive list of partners–including Silicon Graphics, Alias/Wavefront and Sony Canada.

Algonquin's Telecommunications Centre offers customized training and educational services to meet the needs of the expanding telecommunications industry. In addition to training in such areas as software engineering and microelectronics manufacturing, the Centre excels in training needs analysis, curriculum design, prior learning assessment, flexible delivery options and training evaluation.

Other Centres of Excellence include Training, Language, Hospitality and Health Sciences–all geared to deliver instruction that responds to the needs of these specialized areas.

Algonquin College's strength in curriculum development enables it to respond quickly to changes in all of its sectors. Students benefit from cooperative education in the vast majority of Algonquin's programs, ensuring a practical application of the information they receive in class. The diversity of programs offered creates a broad-based, innovative curriculum, and is supported by a wide array of student services.

Financial Aid offices, the Health Services Clinic, Dental Clinic and Student Centre all help Algonquin's students make the most of their time at the College. Other activities and services include extensive athletics facilities and special programs for international students to help them quickly feel at home.

Algonquin College believes that quality training and education is an investment in the future. By helping both students and organizations meet the challenges of today and tomorrow, at home and around the world, it is achieving its vision to be "the trainer of choice." ■

One of Algonquin College's Centres of Excellence, the Telecommunications Centre, offers customized training and education services for the innovative telecommunications industry.

The state-of-the-art Media Centre at Algonquin College offers advanced industry-standard training for the high-technology industry in media programs such as digital publishing and animation.

Future Ottawa: A Community Partnership

*A*s it approaches the 21st century, the Ottawa region has taken giant steps to becoming a thriving business centre and favourite tourist destination. Helping to direct this transformation is Future Ottawa, a marketing support program which unites regional efforts to promote the Ottawa region to the world.

**Ottawa: A world-class capital.
Photo by Malak.**

At the core of Future Ottawa are the organizations that represent the broad economic interests of the community: the Ottawa-Carleton Economic Development Corporation (OCEDCO), the Ottawa-Carleton Board of Trade, the Ottawa Carleton Research Institute (OCRI), the Ottawa Life Sciences Council (OLSC) and the Ottawa Tourism and Convention Authority (OTCA), municipalities, business organizations and the greater community.

Ottawa-Carleton Economic Development Corporation (OCEDCO)

OCEDCO unites the public and private sectors in helping to shape the Ottawa region's economy. It is a catalyst and facilitator for a wide range of economic development initiatives. Its goal is to promote balanced, diverse and sustainable economic growth to enable the Ottawa region to become one of the best places in the world in which to live, work, visit, invest in and do business.

Its priorities are to stimulate the growth of local businesses; assist in the formation of viable new businesses; attract investment, economic activity and businesses to the region; and to build suitable partnerships.

OCEDCO focuses on provision of data and information for business decision-making, services for entrepreneurs, matching of local opportunities to capital and attraction of strategic companies and investments. With its mandate to strengthen external marketing of the region, it works closely with a broad cross-section of private sector companies, advancing economic growth.

Members and volunteers underpin OCEDCO's task forces and committees, placing it among the leaders in economic development practice.

The Ottawa Carleton Research Institute (OCRI)

"Connecting ideas with people, and people with ideas." The Ottawa region is Canada's high-technology centre of excellence, with more than 700 companies involved in R&D and manufacturing in growth sectors such as telecommunications, multimedia and information technologies.

Within this environment, OCRI builds on the strengths of the region to advance technology research and development through collaboration with industries, colleges, universities and government laboratories.

OCRI is a not-for-profit institute supported by more than 240 members. They include large corporations and research laboratories, small and medium-sized technology companies and users, regional government, post-secondary academic institutions and private individuals.

OCRI offers its members an impressive suite of collaborative programs, business services, and networking opportunities.

OCRI's goals are:

• to increase interaction among people from educational institutions, government and industry to enhance the effectiveness of R&D in the region;

• to assist in expanding the resources available for research and development within the region;

• to promote the development of the region in the high-technology sector; and

• to take a leadership role in developing the region's high-technology infrastructure.

The Ottawa Life Sciences Council (OLSC)

The life sciences industry, encompassing biotechnology, medical technology and health-related systems, is one of this region's most important new knowledge-based sectors. It has built upon, and drawn from the top-flight expertise in the region's 24 hospital/university-based and government research institutes. In 1997, there were dozens of new life sciences companies in Ottawa employing some 2,000 people directly, and 18,000 including the public sector, making Ottawa one of Canada's top centres for life sciences technology development and commercialization.

The Ottawa Life Sciences Council was established in 1993 to stimulate the growth of this sector through strategic planning, collaboration with other lead organizations in the field, fundraising and by championing its accomplishments in Canada and internationally. The Council initiated a successful annual life sciences conference to showcase innovative research and facilitate networking.

To accommodate this rapidly growing sector, the provincial government, the City of Ottawa and local health care institutions have established a 22-acre Ottawa Life Sciences Technology Park adjoining a major hospital-research institute complex known as the Ottawa Health Sciences Centre.

The Ottawa Tourism and Convention Authority (OTCA)

From pomp and history to beauty and sophistication, Ottawa has all the ingredients for a top visitors' destination. It is a magnificent national capital with waterways and vast green spaces, unique heritage sites, superb museums, a lively cultural life, renowned festivals and year-round recreational sports. In fact, tourism ranks among the region's major industries, directly supporting some 12,000 jobs. In 1996, the city welcomed over 5 million tourists who spent $634 million in the National Capital Region. Visitors who come to Ottawa for business meetings and conventions are an important segment of this industry. Convention delegates spend more than $900 per party on average, giving a $190-million boost to local businesses and suppliers.

The Ottawa Tourism and Convention Authority, sustained by over 400 members, works with local businesses to promote and develop tourism in the region. It accomplishes its mission through partnerships with the tourism, business and government communities; intensive marketing locally, across Canada and throughout

the world; many special programs and projects with members; and initiatives like developing the concept of Future Ottawa as a way of collaborating with the other economic development organizations here.

The Ottawa-Carleton Board of Trade

Since its founding in 1857, the Ottawa-Carleton Board of Trade has committed itself to promoting and extending the community's trade and commerce.

Today, the Board's membership and concerns encompass the entire metropolitan Ottawa region. As the only region-wide, independent business organization, the board speaks on behalf of the business community on issues like taxation, regulation, balanced budgets and transportation.

The Board's accomplishments demonstrate the depth of its commitment. In 1910, it helped save the Rideau Canal, while in the 1950s and 1960s, it launched two of the region's most popular tourist attractions, the Canadian Tulip Festival and Parliament Hill's Changing of the Guard Ceremony. It also played a strong role in the creation of the Sparks Street Mall and has campaigned tirelessly for strong education facilities, transportation links and responsible government at all levels.

The Board of Trade continues to protect the interests of local business and improve the region's business climate through its committees, task forces and the research it sponsors. It also serves its members by providing opportunities to network and generate new business contacts, participate in professional development and benefit from money-saving group discount programs. In every way, the Ottawa-Carleton Board of Trade serves as the voice of business in the Ottawa region. ■

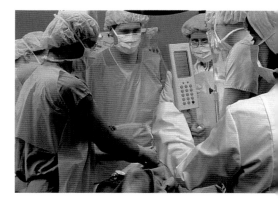

Ottawa is home to a number of industry giants in high technology and life sciences.

Ottawa is emerging as one of the best places in the world to live, work, visit, invest and do business.

Université d'Ottawa / University of Ottawa

For nearly 150 years, the University of Ottawa has been uniquely positioned at the juncture of English and French Canada in the National Capital Region. It is the oldest and largest bilingual university in North America.

As Ottawa-Carleton's eighth largest employer, it has 3,000 staff members and generates more than $400 million annually for the community. The student body comprises some 24,000 full-time and part-time students of whom 37 per cent are French-speaking, the highest proportion on a bilingual campus in Canada.

Founded in 1848 by a Roman Catholic religious order, the University was originally a liberal arts college. It gained its present secular status in 1965, when granted a provincial charter as Université d'Ottawa/University of Ottawa, and given the dual mandate of furthering bilingualism in Canada and developing French culture in Ontario. Over the years, the University's distinct character has evolved in a multicultural setting where students from many ethnic and cultural backgrounds live and study in both French and English.

As a college, the University began conferring undergraduate degrees in 1872 and advanced degrees in 1875. Today it offers a full range of academic and professional programs with some 120 undergraduate majors and concentrations, and graduate programs leading to master's and doctoral degrees in most disciplines. Most programs are given in French and English, and it confers about 6,000 degrees annually.

The University boasts various interdisciplinary institutes and centres in addition to its nine faculties: administration, arts, education, engineering, health sciences, law, medicine, science and social sciences. It has also established important programs in cooperative and distance education, programs with affiliated local teaching hospitals, and on-site degree studies with the region's major high-technology firms.

Innovative educational ventures initiated by the University have broadened the horizons of students in remote parts of Canada and abroad. For example, French-speaking Ontario students can take a wide variety of undergraduate and graduate courses through a University of Ottawa-centered distance education network. The University also offers executives an Ottawa-based MBA program and a similar program in Hong Kong.

Its location in the national capital has enabled both students and faculty to benefit from extraordinary research resources, and to advance Canadian scholarship and technology worldwide. On the international level, the University has more than 100 bilateral agreements with governments, institutes and universities around the world. Many provide for student/faculty exchanges and academic partnerships.

The University has a research budget of $57 million (1995-96) with $40 million allocated to medicine, science and engineering. Scientists at the University have done ground-breaking work in the neurosciences, molecular genetics and cancer research, chemistry and biology. Telecommunications and software engineering and environmental engineering are also areas of research strength. In the other faculties, exceptional work is being done in business and trade law; technology policy, management and transfer; human rights research and education; and in psychology.

In short, Ottawa University plays a central role in the intellectual, social and economic life of Ottawa-Carleton, and is a distinguished and active member of the national and international academic communities. ∎

Over the years, the University's distinct character has evolved in a multicultural setting where students from many ethnic and cultural backgrounds live and study in both French and English.

The University's location in the national capital has enabled both students and faculty to benefit from extraordinary research resources, and to advance Canadian scholarship and technology worldwide.

La Cité collégiale

*L*a Cité collégiale, Ontario's first French-language college of applied arts and technology, serves over 10,000 students on a scenic, $100-million state-of-the-art campus in Ottawa. With an emphasis on specialized training for today's labour market, the college offers more than 75 post-secondary diploma programs, as well as some 500 training courses and activities in a French-speaking environment.

The college's outstanding facilities, its reputation as a dynamic and innovative teaching institution and its superb location in the national capital are major drawing cards for those who wish to pursue their studies in French. As one of Canada's largest French-language technological colleges outside Quebec, *La Cité collégiale* attracts bilingual students from throughout Eastern Ontario, as well as Quebec, New Brunswick and Western Canada.

Before *La Cité collégiale* was established, some 1,600 Ontario students were studying in French at local English-language institutions. When *La Cité collégiale* opened its doors at a temporary location in September 1990, it drew 2,300 full-time students. The new 58-acre campus was inaugurated in October 1995, and by 1997, enrollment totalled 3,600 full-time and 6,500 part-time students. The college also serves Hawkesbury and Cornwall through adult education activities and distance learning.

The college's post-secondary programs include business administration, commerce, electronics, environment and forestry, general and vocational training, housing and design, hotel and restaurant industries, computers, mechanics, media, health and legal services.

To a large degree, *La Cité collégiale's* success is linked to its partnership with the public and private sectors in Ottawa-Carleton. More than 500 employers from the region are on its advisory committees to ensure that programs are attuned to the job market. In co-op placements, apprenticeships and community entrepreneurship programs, students can hone their skills in the workplace. For example, media students have worked with Radio-Canada staff to produce provincial newscasts in French. Computer students, in a collaborative effort with Industry Canada, have instructed hundreds of entrepreneurs on how to use the Internet for business. The college trains apprentices in trades ranging from pastry making and hairdressing, to roofing and industrial mechanics.

In addition to its post-secondary programs, and courses for those who wish to change careers, the college offers professional development workshops to business owners and the general community through its Centre for Professional Development. College staff tailor the content to suit corporate or public sector clients in French or English.

La Cité collégiale also operates a resource centre for entrepreneurs, serving French-speaking clients in five Ontario municipalities. Here individuals starting a small business can get practical advice, mentoring, help in developing a business plan and access to workshops on a range of relevant topics.

Although its first commitment is to meet the needs of Eastern Ontario's French-speaking community and other Canadians, *La Cité collégiale* welcomes students from La Francophonie, 49 countries whose populations are primarily French-speaking. The college maintains student-exchange programs with a variety of European educational institutions. It also sends assistance to foreign educational institutions needing support in technology, the sciences, management and teaching. ■

La Cité collégiale's **$100-million high-tech campus provides quality education and training to more than 10,000 students from Ontario and around the world.**

La Cité collégiale, c'est:

- Un collège à la fine pointe de la technologie
- Au coeur de la capitale nationale du Canada
- 500 programmes et activités de formation
- 100 laboratoires hautement spécialisés
- 75 programmes postsecondaires à temps plein
- Plus de 10 000 apprenants et apprenantes
- Un univers de services

In October 1995, *La Cité collégiale* **inaugurated its new campus in the presence of the Right Honourable Jean Chrétien, prime minister of Canada (center), Normand Fortier, chairman of the board of governors (left), and Andrée Lortie, president of the college (right).**

The Public Service Alliance of Canada

Public Service Alliance of Canada Headquarters

Improved employment security was a major objective of the 1991 PSAC national general strike.

The Public Service Alliance of Canada is a national trade union representing men and women in approximately 170 bargaining units across Canada, and in Canadian embassies and trade missions around the world. In the Ottawa-Carleton region, the Alliance represents about 45,000 federal public service employees and their families. One of Canada's largest unions, it is affiliated with the Canadian Labour Congress and the Public Services International.

The Alliance was founded in 1966 when the Civil Service Federation of Canada and the Civil Service Association of Canada merged in order to present a united front to the Government of Canada. The government was then in the process of granting collective bargaining rights to federal public service employees through the Public Service Staff Relations Act.

While the majority of the Alliance membership is still composed of people working for the federal and territorial governments, many other groups of workers have voted to join the union. They work for diverse employers, ranging from courier companies to casinos, universities to transition houses. Alliance members may work as clerks, communicators, tradespeople, technicians, administrators, enforcement officers, firefighters and food inspectors. From remote Arctic weather stations to downtown high-rise office buildings, Alliance members live and work in most Canadian communities.

The Alliance provides a myriad of services to its members, including representation in collective bargaining, or in redress procedures that have even led to the Supreme Court of Canada. It also has an extensive leadership training program that provides workplace representatives with the tools they need to ensure a safe, healthy and discrimination-free workplace.

In its 30-year history, the Alliance has won many victories with the support of its membership. The union has achieved breakthroughs in almost every area of bargaining, including compensation, job security, hours of work, maternity and parental leave, classification and technological change.

There have been a number of strikes in the Alliance's history of striving for advances for Canadian workers. In 1980, the 60,000 members of the Clerical and Regulatory Group, most of whom were women, successfully undertook their first strike action for equal pay, maternity leave and reasonable pay rates. Since then, women members have helped the Alliance take a leadership role on equality issues within the Canadian labour movement and around the world.

In 1991, more than 100,000 Alliance members took to the streets in a national general strike to protest the Canadian government's actions toward public services and workers who provided them. An Act of Parliament ended the strike, ordering public service employees back to work. However, one of the strike's major objectives, improved employment security, was agreed to by the parties involved.

This strike was unique in that the union tied its demands to an exigency that would protect vital public services for all Canadians, reflecting the labour movement's concern for the wider community. Throughout its history, the Alliance has strongly supported social and economic justice as well as equality. It has defended these principles for union members, their communities and all Canadians. ■

Carleton University

Local community leaders created Carleton University in 1942 as a small evening college to serve the educational needs of the region. Carleton is the only university in Ontario history whose founding was not financed by either church or government grants, but rather through student fees, community fund-raising and partnerships.

As Ottawa prospered, Carleton expanded to serve its needs. The university's entrepreneurial spirit, openness to the community and unique academic programs have created opportunities for three generations of students. Today, Carleton's wide range of programs in over 50 academic disciplines attracts more than 18,000 students to its scenic campus.

Carleton's evolution is a story of stellar accomplishment in a changing environment. After the Second World War, the federal government was the region's growth industry. To serve the educational needs of public servants, Carleton developed Canada's first public administration program, superb departments of economics and political science, and the distinguished Norman Paterson School of International Affairs. In 1944, it laid the foundation for Canada's first School of Journalism, with courses taught by eminent journalists covering the nation's political affairs. These initiatives formed the basis for Carleton's national reputation for excellence in public affairs, management and social sciences.

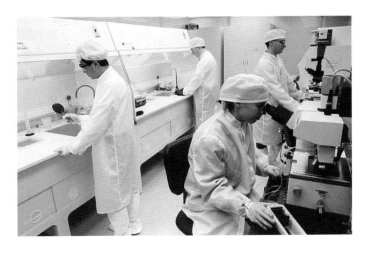

In the 1950s and 1960s, Ottawa became an incubator for research and development in science and technology. The National Research Council (NRC) and the Defence Research Board established world-renowned laboratories here, and Carleton University's science and engineering curricula grew alongside them. The university now offers science and engineering degrees from the bachelor's to the doctoral level, including degrees in such in-demand fields as systems, computer, aerospace and electrical engineering, computer science, medical physics, biochemistry and environmental science. Its earth sciences program is the only one in Canada top-rated in both petroleum and hard-rock mining geology. Upon the NRC's closing its high-energy particle physics lab in 1990, Carleton created the self-sustaining Centre for Research in Particle Physics, initially staffed by former NRC scientists.

The shift of the region's economic base from public service to the advanced technology sector in the early 1980s provided a wealth of new opportunities for Carleton's expanding programs. Its computer and systems engineering program was a first for Ontario, as was the industrial research chair in computer science founded in 1996. Carleton engineering and computer science faculty now hold seven research chairs co-sponsored by industry and government.

The relationships and partnerships the university has developed with the local high-tech community provide many mutual advantages, including research collaboration and work and research placements for students. Over 90 per cent of the region's high-tech companies hire Carleton graduates.

Similarly in public affairs and social sciences, Carleton University produces graduates who excel in the work world. Carleton graduates of economics, sociology and statistics programs top the recruiting list of the Public Service of Canada. Carleton's School for Studies in Art and Culture boasts unique programs in Canadian art history, film studies and music. Participating students can work in the capital's national cultural institutions, gaining credits and on-the-job experience. Carleton's prolific history department tops off a comprehensive range of undergraduate and graduate studies with doctoral programs in women's and Canadian history, while the new College of Humanities attracts the country's top students with its rigorous liberal arts program.

With its extraordinary range of degree programs leading to careers in today's most sought-after fields, Carleton University proudly offers "Education for Life." ■

Carleton University's scenic campus is located just 10 minutes from Parliament Hill. Photo by Canadian Aerial Photo Corporation.

Carleton's Microelectronics Fabrication Facility, the only complete fabrication facility at a Canadian university, provides outstanding research opportunities for both undergraduate and graduate students.

Photo by Ari Tapiero

CHAPTER FIFTEEN

The Marketplace, Hospitality & Attractions

The Corel Centre and the Ottawa Senators

Hockey legends colour Ottawa's history, just as Ottawa figures large in the sport's origins. One source puts hockey's beginning on the frozen Ottawa River on Christmas Day 1852, the product of a "shinny" match between Bytown and New Edinburgh, both of which are now Ottawa neighbourhoods.

January 17, 1996: They shoot, they score! The Ottawa Senators' first goal in the Corel Centre, their new home, took place in front of a sold-out crowd.

Born in Ottawa or not, hockey caught the imagination of the entire community, selling out games and prompting Governor General and Ottawa resident Lord Stanley to order in 1892 a gold-lined silver bowl on an ebony base: the Lord Stanley Cup, the championship which still fires the imaginations of hockey fans across North America.

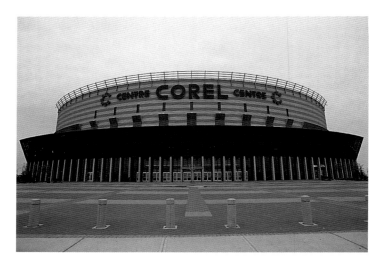

The Corel Centre is 600,000 square feet of dazzling versatility. From the energy of NHL hockey to the rhythm of music superstars to the artistry of professional figure skating, it brings the world to Ottawa.

But the Depression saw the early Ottawa Senators hockey club—winners of nine Stanley Cups—fold. For 60 years, they remained absent from Ottawa.

That ended October 8, 1992, when the puck dropped on the first game of the Ottawa Senators' expansion franchise. The Senators won 5 to 3 against the Montreal Canadiens that night, with the Civic Centre's packed-to-the-rafters crowd giving an overwhelming welcome to NHL hockey back in Ottawa.

Just over three years later, the Senators played their first game in the $200-million Corel Centre, then named the Palladium. Ottawa not only had its NHL hockey team back, but it also had North America's newest and best sports and entertainment facility. The home of the Ottawa Senators, the Corel Centre takes its name from Corel Corporation, the powerhouse high-tech software company that has made an indelible impression upon the region's corporate and social landscape with its unwavering support of community activities, charitable works and sporting events. The high-technology link is fitting for a world-class facility that is in itself the most advanced building of its kind on the continent. From computer-engineered sightlines to hand-held wireless devices for concession ordering, from the computer-controlled climate to its state-of-the-art electronics, the Corel Centre has more in common with the booming high-tech sector than its location in Kanata, just 15 minutes from downtown Ottawa.

Excitement at Every Level

The Corel Centre also offers business and government a place to meet, to conduct business and to forge new ties. From top high-tech leaders to Prime Minister Jean Chrétien, the nation's leaders are finding the Corel Centre's facilities second to none.

Beyond its 18,500 plush, cushioned seats and its 150 executive suites lies an unrivaled range of services. Four restaurants offer experiences from fine dining to sports-oriented Marshy's, the Hard Rock Cafe's rock and roll and the Penalty Box with view and gourmet sandwich bar. Business and social entertaining is accommodated through corporate boxes, a banquet hall and meeting rooms, all of which enjoy catering under the direction of the Corel Centre's chef, Orazio LaManna, 1996 Chef of the Year. Also under the five-acre Corel Centre roof are the Ottawa-Carleton west-region YMCA-YWCA, a sports medicine and physiotherapy centre and the offices of the Kanata Chamber of Commerce.

Kanata is Iroquois for "the meeting place," a fitting comment on the Corel Centre's capacity for bringing people and events together. The building's design incorporates unsurpassed acoustic characteristics, making it the perfect setting for major concerts like Bryan Adams, Céline Dion and Alanis Morissette. In addition to NHL hockey, the Corel Centre's 600,000 square feet of enclosed space hosts such events as Walt Disney's World On Ice, the Harlem Globetrotters and professional figure skating tours.

Sensational Senators

Of course, the Ottawa Senators remain at the heart of the Corel Centre, playing half of their 82 regular season games on home ice, thrilling fans with hard-hitting, top quality hockey. NHL playoff action is now a spring fixture on the Ottawa entertainment calendar.

But the Senators are just as important to the community off the ice. Both the franchise and individual players sponsor special programs to support local charities. "Sens at Your Service," organized by the Senators Wives Foundation, features five-star dining with the players as star waiters. The Senators' wives also organize the Senators Carnival, which brings the team closer to its fans through a fun-filled event that features oppor-tunities to meet the players among its activities.

The Annual Charity Golf Classic raises funds for regional youth charities, while Marsh's Minors gives minor hockey team players the chance to raise funds for their team travel. Ticket holders unable to attend home games can donate their tickets to a local charity through a unique Senators Ticket Donation program.

Travelling Together

The Corel Centre and the Ottawa Senators take these links to their community seriously. The road back to NHL hockey was a long and twisting one, a journey undertaken by a few key visionaries . . . and an entire community caught up in the Canadian dream that is professional hockey.

The spark flamed in 1988, when Terrace Investments owner Bruce Firestone recognized that Ottawa could be part of the NHL's anticipated expansion and developed a strategy to bring back the Senators. A central part of which was a new home for the team. The community rallied around the idea, including SHL Systemhouse founder Rod

Bryden. But the December 6, 1990, NHL announcement that Ottawa had won the Senators was only the beginning of a fight to bring the team to life.

Two vital companies came to the Senators' aid: Ogden Corporation, respected arena managers based in New York, lent the franchise financial support and their vast expertise operating sports and entertainment facilities; and S.C. Stormont Corporation, Rod Bryden's investment company, set to work organizing the financing for the building itself. Through environmental hearings, unravelling bank syndicates, and government promises lost through election turnarounds, the players persevered . . . and won.

Today the investment of a third of a billion dollars in the Corel Centre and the Senators has established a centre of sports and entertainment excellence that is a fitting neighbour for the world-class technology industries that are driving the dynamic economy of the Ottawa region. ■

Founder, Dr. Bruce Firestone, and current owner, Roderick Bryden, drop the ceremonial first puck before the first-ever Ottawa Senators game at the Corel Centre on January 17, 1996.

It's strategy time in the Senators' scrum as the team treats fans to more fast-paced, hard-hitting NHL action.

Bayshore Shopping Centre

Bayshore Shopping Centre is ready for the 21st century. From its strategic location in Ottawa-Carleton's west end, the mall has a unique vantage point on the future.

Bright, clean, accessible facilities; features for families; upbeat music through a good quality sound system; and 165 businesses offering an attractive mix of products and services that its customers want: Bayshore offers not just a great location in which to shop, but a great feeling about shopping.

The popular shopping centre plans on carrying that feeling right through the millennium.

Bayshore opened its first two floors in 1973, expanding to three floors in 1987 and designating the third level as fashion's exclusive domain. The fashion concentration worked well, and added another feature to the one-stop shopping for which Bayshore was already recognized. Now more than ever, the centre is much more than a mall; it's a destination in itself.

Anchored by the Bay, Eaton's and Zellers, Bayshore also offers a Your Independent Grocer grocery store, making it one of the few enclosed shopping centres to truly offer every possible purchase in one place, from furniture to fashion to food.

Recent additions to the Bayshore mix focus on families, making shopping more fun for both parents and children. Port Pizzazz, for instance, is new, but catching on fast. Operated by Gym Jam, this lively, innovative child care facility is filled with happy children enjoying the slides and tunnels of its play structures or making imaginative crafts. Parents, meanwhile, are browsing, relaxing or taking care

Bayshore Shopping Centre's focus on families makes shopping fun for parents and children alike.

Conveniently located in Ottawa-Carleton's west end, Bayshore Shopping Centre takes pride in creating a bright, clean, pleasant ambience for its customers.

of business, secure in the knowledge that Port Pizzazz is supervised, safe and non-competitive. If they are needed, parents are only a pager signal away.

For families shopping together, the first level's family washroom offers expanded facilities that are a boon to parents juggling packages, strollers and children.

The attention paid to family shoppers clearly demonstrates how Bayshore serves its market in more ways than simply offering an enclosed building for shopping convenience. It listens to its customers, responds quickly to their expectations and adjusts the merchandise mix to fit their needs.

It's also making the centre a community cornerstone. In 1996 alone, 77 non-profit groups raised $90,000 in the mall to aid their important work, a record that Bayshore is both proud of and committed to continuing. In addition to the charitable organizations it assists, the centre is finding special ways to acknowledge its customers' different interests.

A newly developed Community Access Centre offers local non-profit organizations an opportunity to promote awareness and raise funds. At the customer service kiosk, shoppers can obtain strollers and wheelchairs, find updates on store or mall promotions and purchase Bayshore Shopping Centre gift certificates.

Features like these keep customers coming back, again and again. Bayshore's resulting strong sales performance is reflected in its anchor stores, which perform well above their respective chain averages, and in the healthy cross-over shopping between major stores and smaller boutiques that a recent mall survey revealed. The shopping centre also works hard to maintain a welcoming ambience for visitors and shoppers, many of whom pass by the mall every day on their way to work.

If location offers the secret to success, then Bayshore has a distinct advantage. Its 26-acre site lies next to Highway 417, the major east-west route through Ottawa-Carleton, and in close proximity to Highway 416, which extends south through the region's greenbelt. Highway 417 provides unrivalled visibility, with the cheerful Bayshore sign greeting passersby from both directions, while Richmond Road gives the centre great north-south exposure.

By car or via OC Transpo's frequent bus service, Bayshore Shopping Centre is easily reached–by design. A large, 4,000-space parking lot with clear entrances and exits and smooth traffic flow complements the fast access from all points of the compass.

The building itself offers good accessibility as

well. Hassle-free to get into and out of, it's also easy to navigate once inside. A single large aisle provides logical, efficient walking patterns for customers, while ensuring good frontage for stores and services. Strategically placed maps help shoppers quickly locate specific destinations within the mall.

Once customers arrive in the mall, the building's architecture ensures bright, natural light, while an interior design that includes the lush greens of real foliage brings the softness of nature inside, even when the weather outside is less than perfect. Very high standards of cleanliness and maintenance add to the atmosphere, giving customers a secure, pleasant environment in which to shop.

Bayshore's trade area is situated south of the Ottawa River in Ontario, and ranges from beyond Orleans in the region's east and points west to Arnprior and southerly towards Perth and Smiths Falls. Falling squarely inside this area are the key western communities of Nepean and Kanata, from which Bayshore draws many of its customers. As a result of the centre's extensive fashion representation and its easy access, Bayshore also has a strong following from residents in downtown Ottawa.

The primary trade area has an average household income that is 17 per cent above the national average, with the shopping centre attracting three key customer segments: suburban affluent, urban young singles, and suburban upscale families.

The store and services mix reflects this population, offering a range of products in Bayshore's 750,000 square feet of leasable space that appeals to everyone from seniors to kids. From home computing to gifts, kitchen specialties to phone centres, sporting goods to books, Bayshore offers both quality and variety.

And with its doors open seven days a week with an attractive, energizing atmosphere, it's no

surprise that the shopping centre is recognized as a top player, in Ottawa and across Canada. Bayshore's excellent sales performance has proven instrumental in attracting top retailers, which, in turn, attract both new and repeat shoppers. Bayshore Shopping Centre's focus on the next century is already creating a winning environment, to the benefit of customers and stores alike. ■

Always in style: Bayshore Shopping Centre has devoted its entire third floor to fashion, earning great reviews from style-conscious customers.

The 165 businesses that call Bayshore Shopping Centre home offer a range of products and services that appeals to everyone: from fashion to food to furniture, it's all here.

Turpin Group Inc.

F ernand Turpin never envisioned Turpin Pontiac Buick GMC to become the largest automotive sales, leasing and automotive repair company in Ottawa-Carleton. His vision was simply to be the best.

With two dealerships in the Ottawa area, Turpin Pontiac Buick GMC and Turpin Saturn Saab Isuzu provide their customers with exactly that: total customer satisfaction, quality service and superior workmanship, in an atmosphere devoted to the highest levels of integrity and business ethics.

The Pontiac-Buick-GMC dealership at 1666 Carling Avenue sits next door to the Saturn-Saab-Isuzu franchise at 1650 Carling, with both locations supported by the Paint and Collision Centre at 1615 Laperriere Avenue.

Although Turpin Group sells and services hundreds of new and used vehicles each year, its top-quality personnel strive to treat each customer like royalty.

"We recognized from the beginning that we had to be different and we had to care for customers," explains Mr. Turpin, whose role as president guides the company and its employees. "We treat the customer as a guest in our place of business."

This owes much to Turpin Group's belief in the strength of its people and in the team atmosphere the company fosters. Fernand Turpin recalls his father telling him that in order to be successful, he had to treat his employees well. "You have to have good people," Turpin says. "You have to be able to motivate them and they have to love working for you."

Top-notch, ongoing training in both customer service and product knowledge and a genuine pleasure in employee success hallmark Turpin's approach. "At one time we were known as a training school," he notes. "To see your employees graduate from your dealership is very gratifying." Some of his employees have since become dealers, including one of Turpin's sons who

now runs a GM dealership in Hawkesbury.

Personnel with 20, 30 and even 40 years of service with the company aren't unusual, a sign of the dedication to both employees and customers that has made Turpin an Ottawa-area business leader.

It could all have been very different. At the age of 20, Fern Turpin was invited to represent Canada in the 1948 Olympics as a member of the Canadian Hockey Team. He chose to establish roots in the business community instead, and says he has no regrets about the route he chose, which led him and two family members to open Turpin Motors in Gatineau.

It was May 1949, and the Texaco service and repair centre grew quickly under the trio's management and their attention to customer satisfaction. When they added new vehicles to their portfolio, they sold approximately 75 in their first year. The Texaco site became a General Motors facility in 1954, when GM offered Mr. Turpin and his brother Roland a Chevrolet-Oldsmobile dealership. The Turpins expanded and redesigned the site to include a one-car showroom, used vehicle department, mechanical and body repairs and genuine GM parts.

Turpin purchased his brother's shares five years later, selling the Gatineau site in 1961 and acquiring a Richmond Road Pontiac-Buick-GMC location that he renamed Turpin Pontiac Buick Ltd. The landmark 1666 Carling location came about just five years afterward, when Turpin needed more space to provide the level of

The Turpin Pontiac Buick GMC facility provides both customers and employees with the most modern and convenient of dealership amenities, including an impressive 20-car showroom.

The Turpin Saturn Saab Isuzu facility incorporated all elements of the Saturn RED program. Opened in January 1997, Retail Environmental Design (RED) is a concept derived entirely with the customer in mind.

customer service he considered essential for continued growth. He designed and supervised the new facility's construction himself, something

he enjoys. "If I hadn't been in the automobile business I guess I would have been in the construction business, because I've been building all along."

Expansion again became necessary in 1987, resulting in the Laperriere location. The building's renovation added a new section, while its new equipment surpassed industry standards for repairing and painting modern vehicles. Along with auto body repair and paint services, the Paint and Collision Centre handles new vehicle preparation and pre-delivery inspection.

The Saturn-Saab-Isuzu dealership arrived in 1988, housed in a facelifted showroom at 1666 Carling. It found its own home in 1997 in a new facility constructed next door, while 1666 Carling was redesigned to meet GM's high standards for the Pontiac-Buick-GMC dealers Image 2000 program.

All of the facilities offer innovative services focused on the customer: past, present and future. Turpin initiated after-service contact in the Ottawa area, checking with its customers to ensure their satisfaction. It also began a program to invite vehicle buyers back to the dealership shortly after their purchase to learn about the company and meet the technicians and parts people, and it launched "Women's Car Care Clinics," in which female car buyers can visit the dealership to learn about such necessities as maintenance and tire repair.

Fern Turpin has served on many groundbreaking industry groups, recently piloting a GM distance learning course on brakes which linked several technicians from across Canada via satellite with a teacher in Oshawa, Ontario.

This service above and beyond, to customers and to the industry, reflects the way Turpin

operates in the community. Fern Turpin received the 1993 Commemorative Medal for the 125th anniversary of Canadian Confederation in recognition of his active participation with such projects as United Way campaigns, the Children's Hospital of Eastern Ontario Dream of a Lifetime, the Snowsuit Fund and the Elisabeth-Bruyere Health Service Centre.

Such involvement also led to a Silver Award as the Ottawa-Carleton Board of Trade's 1996 Business Person of the Year, the criteria for which include dedication to business development, job creation and expansion, a high regard for business standards and ethics and community involvement.

Turpin Group mirrors these achievements: Turpin Pontiac Buick GMC has won the GM Triple Crown, given to the top 100 dealers across Canada, 15 times in the 19 years GM has offered the award.

"We recognized from the beginning that we had to be different and we had to care for customers. We treat the customer as a guest in our place of business."

Fern Turpin's vision and Turpin Group's high standards explain why so many customers recommend the dealerships to friends and relatives and return over the years to buy successive vehicles from a company they trust. For them, Turpin Group is simply the best. ■

J. Fernand Turpin has enjoyed 46 years of success doing business in the nation's capital. He shows his appreciation by proudly flying the Canadian flag on site.

The Westin Ottawa

Discriminating travellers consistently rank the 484-room Westin Ottawa among Canada's most highly preferred hotels. Part of the Westin family that extends across North America and around the world, The Westin Ottawa–a CAA/AAA Four Diamond Award winner–offers business and leisure travellers an outstanding array of services.

Situated in the same complex as the 85,723-square-foot Ottawa Congress Centre and the 200-plus stores, restaurants and services of the Rideau Centre, the hotel is close to everything that makes Ottawa one of Canada's most popular tourist and convention destinations.

But the location, on the historic Rideau Canal and just a short walk from Parliament Hill, is only the beginning.

Anup Israni, the hotel's director of sales and marketing, explains: "When a Westin guest walks into the lobby, they know exactly what standards to expect. Our goals are to meet–and exceed–their expectations."

With spacious rooms and suites, stunning city views and fresh air vents in every room, The Westin Ottawa surrounds its guests with comfort and style. Guests also enjoy extensive health club facilities, a delicious choice of dining options and specialty services guaranteed to make each stay as productive and pleasant as possible.

Through the Westin's Guest Offices[SM] program, business travellers can choose to combine the efficiency and technology of an office with the unsurpassed comfort and luxury of a private guest room. These rooms feature a multifunction laser printer/fax/copier, speakerphone with data port, printer cables, surge protector and coffee maker. Office supplies are provided, along with an ergonomically designed desk chair and glare-free task lamp, and a full range of guest privileges.

For assistance in planning small meetings–before a guest even arrives at the hotel–Westin One Call[SM] fits the bill. One toll-free call links business travellers to a Westin meetings expert who can schedule, organize, price and manage every detail.

Service is streamlined on site as well, with the revolutionary Service Express[SM] concept. Guests dial just one number on their in-room telephone for any and all service requests: from laundry to luggage, one call does it all.

The Westin Premier® program offers Westin guests the most rewarding frequent guest program in the hotel industry. Points are redeemable for a multitude of award options, from room upgrades and free hotel nights to week-long vacations with airfare.

And children are welcomed through the Westin Kids Club,[SM] which extends far beyond babysitting services and children's menus to include advance room set-up, preferred restaurant reservations and special services for infants.

Throughout the operation, seamless integration of cutting-edge technology allows The Westin Ottawa to track guest preferences, speed reservations and check-in, and provide fast, accurate information on Westin Hotels and Resorts worldwide.

"It gives our guests quicker responses and superior service," says Israni. "Along with our strong location and fine amenities, harnessing the power of technology is a key element in The Westin Ottawa's commitment to quality and innovation." ■

Daly's Restaurant is renowned for its fine food, impeccable service and incomparable view overlooking the scenic Rideau Canal.

The Westin Ottawa welcomes business and leisure travellers, offering premier meeting and recreational facilities and a location at the very heart of the city's business and tourist districts.

Cartier Place & Towers Suite Hotels

I n a city teeming with guest venues, it's hard to know which offers the most value for the money, the friendliest staff and the best location.

One that tops the list is the family owned and operated Cartier Place & Towers Suite Hotels, right in the heart of Ottawa at Cooper and Elgin. This suite hotel, just a few minutes away from Parliament Hill, is located in a quiet neighbourhood that borders the Rideau Canal and the trendy boutique area of Elgin Street. The accommodations are spacious studios, one and two bedroom suites, and feature fully equipped kitchens, separate living room and bedrooms. Laundry facilities are conveniently located on guest room floors. The staff is friendly and responsive and the price is just right.

Many of the hotels in the city can make these same claims, of course, but few can equal the Cartier Place's strict attention to detail and outstanding customer service. Many of the guests are repeat clientele or have been referred by word of mouth. Due to its popularity, the hotel runs at 90 per cent occupancy year round.

The management goes the extra distance to ensure the comfort of all visitors, little ones included. Children receive a colouring book and crayons upon check-in, and a welcome basket awaits each guest in his or her suite. Cartier Place also offers families staying with children a games room, complimentary toys, cartoon channel and an outdoor playground with a skating rink in the winter. Upon request, cribs, high chairs and even babysitting services are available.

Adults are treated with the same care. A variety of activities designed to keep them entertained and happy include VIP passes to local nightclubs, discounted sports and event tickets, ski and golf packages, weekly barbecue nights and aerobic classes. The full-service health club, indoor pool complete with pool toys, whirlpool, sauna and outdoor garden and patio are available for the use

The spacious suites have all the conveniences of home ... and a few added touches. Photo by Gordon King.

of guests who want to unwind after a long day. Of course, guests may choose to relax by taking in the fresh air and romantic surroundings on their own private balcony off of their suite.

The banquet rooms feature ceiling-to-floor windows overlooking flowerbed gardens. During the summer months, the gardens surrounding the hotel resemble a Monet painting. Guests can enjoy a delicious meal in this setting on the restaurant's outdoor patio.

The business traveller will discover all the conveniences of the office available upon request, including computer, fax and cellular phone services.

Each guest's individual needs are meticulously recorded in guest history, which automatically enrolls them in the hotel's frequent stay program. Any guest staying with the hotel also receives discounted car rental rates worldwide.

One can easily see how the hotel earned its trademark, "Suite Dreams await you...." ■

Enjoy the indoor pool, whirlpool, sauna, exercise room and outdoor patio complete with children's playground. Photo by Gordon King.

Les Suites Hotel Ottawa

Located downtown in the heart of Ottawa's historical cultural area, Les Suites Hotel opened its doors in 1989 with a new and growing concept in the hotel industry—an all-suite hotel. Since its inception, Les Suites Hotel has become a leader in the Ottawa market and a visible part of the surrounding community.

Catering to small meetings, Les Suites Hotel provides flexibility, convenience and charm. A successful event always includes some free time activities, which are in abundance in the vicinity of Les Suites Hotel. Located just steps away are the Parliament Buildings, Rideau Canal, national museums and the Byward Market—a collection of shops, restaurants and outdoor stalls that contain anything from fresh produce to freshly cut flowers. If shopping is the agenda for the day, the Rideau Centre shopping complex awaits with a selection of over 100 stores and boutiques. Feeling adventurous? A delectable sampling of local cuisine is available at more than 125 restaurants within a six-block radius.

Business and leisure travellers alike find a warm welcome awaiting them at Les Suites Hotel.

Spacious Elegance in a Picture-Perfect Setting

Les Suites Hotel—your home away from home—features elegantly appointed one- and two-bedroom suites with fully equipped kitchens and en suite laundry facilities. The spacious living and dining areas are perfect for working or relaxing. Unwind in the complete recreation facility with indoor pool, sauna and whirlpool. Services include in-room movies, Nintendo, free local calls, free newspapers, voice mail messaging and video express checkout. Treat yourself to a light meal in the Café Expresso, or choose from a variety of grocery items and convenience goods to prepare something within your own suite.

In addition to the workspace advantages that a suite provides, many feature direct data lines, enabling guests to transmit and receive simultaneously.

Business and leisure travellers alike find a warm welcome awaiting them at Les Suites Hotel. The staff takes great pleasure in pampering its guests.

For those travelling to Ottawa for a convention, Les Suites is adjacent to the largest convention facility in the city—the Ottawa Congress Centre. Delegates can attend their meetings while spouses or families enjoy the sites of Ottawa or shopping at the Rideau Centre, Byward Market or Sparks Street Mall. ■

Guests of Les Suites will find it easy to unwind in the hotel's complete recreation facility, with its indoor pool, sauna and whirlpool.

Photo by Ari Tapiero

CHAPTER SIXTEEN

Real Estate &
Construction

Royal LePage Commercial Inc.

Royal LePage Commercial Inc. is the driving force in Ottawa's commercial real estate market. As the largest, most diversified commercial real estate group in Canada's capital, the company leads the market in the varied disciplines which its operations cover.

The Ottawa office of Royal LePage Commercial Inc. offers Ottawa the largest, most diversified commercial real estate group in the area.

For Paul Hindo, vice-president and general manager, it is quite simple; the company's strength lies with its people. "In addition to being probably the best team players in town, most of our people are leaders in their own specialties and in the community," he explains. "In fact, we have more specialists in our office than any comparable organization in Ottawa."

This expertise provides crucial spin-offs for the company's clients, spin-offs that include superior technical support. Royal LePage Commercial Inc. has maintained since 1982 a database which tracks office and industrial vacancy rates—a record no other company can match.

"We have what I believe is the best technical support available," says Hindo. "We have a nationally recognized name, and our data is the standard of the industry."

Royal LePage's Leasing Group maintains an eagle eye on office vacancy rates, offering clients superior technical support and information analysis.

And through its affiliation with Cushman & Wakefield Worldwide, the company offers the world to Ottawa, even as it brings Ottawa to the world. This has translated into a tremendous credibility in the commercial real estate marketplace. The company is one of the most quoted sources in the local news media on commercial real estate matters.

Royal LePage Commercial Inc. offers real estate services in all commercial disciplines, including office leasing, investment commercial sales, industrial sales and leasing, retail, land, multi-residential and hospitality, and strategic advisory services.

It further specializes in the particular needs of high-technology companies, recognizing the significance of the Ottawa area's booming high-technology industry to the local economy. Whether a high-tech firm is looking for clean rooms and low vibration locations for manufacturing, or office space for software development, Royal LePage Commercial Inc. understands its requirements, and can match properties to clients quickly and cost-effectively.

Ottawa's reliance on its historical role as Canada's political centre is decreasing. Instead, its growing reputation as the nation's Silicon Valley North is fuelling real estate activity. With many of the region's high-tech companies doing the lion's share of their business outside Canada, this has served to emphasize what Royal LePage calls the "borderless" aspect of today's real estate industry.

International trade and events affect Canadian companies and, therefore, the Canadian real estate market. Increasing free trade means an increased focus on competitiveness, while international investment plays a significant role in establishing new industries, businesses and manufacturing facilities.

But borders are not restricted to geography. In Ottawa, for instance, the buildings themselves—the very bricks and mortar of the real estate market—are finding their uses redefined in the face of changing government priorities. As the federal government continues to reduce its budgetary spending—and, therefore, its office space—high-technology and quasi-government agencies are filling the gap, often necessitating fundamental changes in building use and construction.

And as the Ottawa region decides where and how to grow, owners are redeveloping buildings traditionally viewed as office and industrial spaces into recreational and residential facilities, with outstanding results.

Royal LePage Commercial Inc. stays one step ahead of these market developments, using its relationship with Cushman & Wakefield Worldwide–an alliance of seven of the world's leading real estate service firms–to provide a unique window on the world. A founding member of Cushman & Wakefield Worldwide, the company can bring to its clients the advantages of belonging to an international network of more than 100 offices in 31 countries.

In addition, the company's parent, Royal LePage, has provided residential and commercial real estate services since 1913, and now employs more than 6,000 people in over 200 residential and commercial brokerage, professional services and affiliate offices across Canada. Royal LePage Commercial Inc., which draws from the strategic and advisory resources of its parent to the benefit of its clients, has itself operated in Ottawa for over 25 years.

In that time, the company has proven over and again its commitment to its clients, and to the area at large. The team philosophy within the company extends as well to the relationship it develops with its clients. The only firm in the area that can provide comprehensive brokerage services, Royal LePage Commercial Inc. combines residential, property management, leasing and selling services in one location.

The Retail Group is just one of the areas in which Royal LePage Commercial Inc. offers clients "one-stop shopping," combining key services in one convenient location.

Staying ahead of changes in the marketplace allows the Commercial/Investment/Industrial Sales Group to serve its clients' diverse needs.

"That convenience is very beneficial to a client," says Hindo. "We're committed to providing our clients with the services they require to completely meet their real estate needs. We act as an extension of their own company, providing the same top-quality service they would expect from a real estate department that was their own."

The company's high degree of repeat business and its position of respect within the community speak to the success of this attitude. It isn't surprising to find that the company which operates so in tune with the community, also prides itself in giving back.

"Ottawa is a wonderful city," explains Hindo. "And part of what makes it so special is community involvement at all levels."

Again, Royal LePage and its employees play an active role in this regard. Just one example of this is a simple golf tournament in support of the Ottawa Regional Cancer Centre (ORCC). The annual event has become one of the most successful corporate golf tournaments in the area, selling out within a couple of weeks of its yearly announcement. Since its inception, over $60,000 in donations have flowed to the ORCC.

Royal LePage Commercial Inc. also contributes to the business community in which it operates, participating in such organizations as the Ottawa-Carleton Economic Development Corporation, the Building Owners and Managers Association, and the Ottawa-Carleton Board of Trade.

Staying in touch with the community is just one way that Royal LePage Commercial Inc. maintains the dynamic, creative atmosphere on which its clients rely. As the economy continues to evolve both internationally and locally, Royal LePage Commercial Inc. will be there with it, providing its clients with leading-edge information and unsurpassed service. ∎

Minto Developments Inc.

Over the last 40-plus years, Minto has built more homes in the Ottawa-Carleton region than any other company. It is also the largest private residential landlord in the city. Company-wide, it has built more than 45,000 homes and manages approximately 15,000 homes and over 2 million square feet of commercial space, plus a 418-room all-suite hotel. Minto isn't just building the bricks and mortar of the community, however; it's building the spirit, as well.

Minto takes great pride in designing communities that retain their appeal years after the day they open, and in creating innovative developments that offer the optimum combination of function and graceful living.

"We're very proud of our part in the growth and development of the region," says President Roger Greenberg. "We've long cherished our ability to plan for the future, to be a progressive company. And we're vitally interested in this region's economic and social well-being."

Minto's part in the community began in 1955, when four brothers founded a company with the intention of building homes for Ottawa families. Within four years, the company was building 1,000 homes in the city, progress that continued through the 1950s and 1960s.

Minto Developments Inc. builds long-term value into every development project in its portfolio with effective, hands-on management—a commitment that earned Minto's Enterprise Building a Canada-wide award of excellence.

A second generation is now at the helm of Minto, which has expanded to include branches in Toronto and southeast Florida, all the while maintaining a strong presence in the Ottawa area. Its residential expertise focuses on the belief that development success depends on paying special attention to master planning complete communities. A single vision guides each project the company undertakes, while house designs feature comfort and function for today and for the future.

Minto now offers a wide spectrum of homes throughout the Ottawa region, affording opportunities for first-time, move-up and move-down buyers alike. Its designs include virtually every type of dwelling found in North America. All communities are planned using the same goals of quality and value, and benefit from Minto's sensitivity to the natural landscape surrounding the buildings.

From top architectural and design talent to experienced property managers, the team at Minto is focused on working together, communicating and finding better ways of doing business. And that team includes Minto's customers. "We've always been dedicated to innovation, integrity and the pursuit of excellence," says Greenberg. "But the best thing we do is listen."

Regular newsletters containing community and company news as well as post-occupancy surveys reinforce the two-way communication between Minto and its customers. Youth drop-in centres and seniors groups in several of its rental developments have become an integral part of the larger community, thanks to Minto's initiative and the residents' participation.

"We promote very strongly the philosophy that we have to give back to the community that has given us so much," notes Greenberg.

The company's industry-wide recognition reflects this attitude, with Minto earning Ontario's highest rating each and every year for new home after-sales service. For its combination of excellence in original construction, design and ongoing management, Minto's 300,000-square-foot Enterprise Building won the 1995 National Toby Award for Office Building of the Year from the Building Owners and Managers Association.

These are two fitting rewards for Minto, a company whose concern for the community and commitment to quality show in every one of its projects, both commercial and residential. ■

Minto Place Suite Hotel

A home away from home awaits travellers at Minto Place Suite Hotel Ottawa, just blocks from Parliament Hill.

Providing that sense of home is the hotel's biggest success story, says general manager E. Harry Dugal, helping the hotel earn the coveted CAA/AAA Four Diamond Award, and a reputation as Ottawa's premier luxury all-suite hotel.

Offering travellers double the space of a conventional hotel room, the hotel's 418 tastefully appointed suites feature such advantages as fully-equipped kitchens, en-suite laundry facilities, and living and dining areas for business and entertaining.

These advantages come with a location in Minto Place, Ottawa's innovative, multi-use complex in the city's central business and shopping district.

Dugal explains that Minto Place's 30 shops and services and two office towers allow guests to do all the things they would at home. Convenience isn't the only benefit. The Minto Place facility also provides guests with exemplary security, a feature that Dugal says appeals particularly to the hotel's female guests.

Security begins with the Marlock Control System, in which each room key becomes an individually coded security program in its own right. Security and fire alarm systems are monitored on-site, 24 hours a day. Trained staff patrol the premises, including the underground garage, where emergency stations allow guests who need assistance to pull an alarm and speak directly to a security guard.

Of course, the suites themselves offer privacy in their set-up, with entertaining areas discreetly separated from sleeping areas, and comfortable kitchens and room service eliminating the need for dining out alone.

Minto Place Suite Hotel focuses the same care on its corporate services, which include a full-service seminar and conference centre, and direct access to office support. For its corporate guests the hotel provides a variety of bright, comfortable and soundproof banquet and meeting rooms with internally wired translation, audio-visual outlets and superb catering.

History merges seamlessly with modern technology in the Lord Minto Boardroom which features the 14-foot walnut and mahogany boardroom table that once graced the Railway Boardroom on Parliament Hill. With its location on the top floor of the hotel, the Boardroom offers special meetings an elegant setting with capital views of the city.

For guests ready to disconnect, Minto Place Suite Hotel boasts a well-equipped, complimentary pool and fitness centre containing state-of-the-art health and spa facilities.

Minto Place Suite Hotel features all the comforts and conveniences of a home away from home in its spacious, fully-equipped suites— at prices that invite comparison.

And Noah's tempts both groups and single travellers with a mouth-watering menu guaranteed both fresh and flexible. Whether it's the casual chic of the bar or the quiet ambience of the sunken dining rooms, Noah's sets the atmosphere with whimsical animal art, soft sculptured chairs and friendly servers.

In fact, says Dugal, it's the service guests find throughout Minto Place Suite Hotel that keeps people coming back. "Guests are not room numbers; they're individuals," he says. "The hotel's design serves the corporate and long-term stay markets very effectively, but it's our attention to the needs of our guests that really sets us apart." ■

Located 20 minutes from Ottawa's International Airport and just blocks from Parliament Hill, Minto Place Suite Hotel is the city's premier all-suite hotel.

Photo by Ari Tapiero

Bibliography

Bagnall, James. "Newbridge to double by 2001." The *Ottawa Citizen*, July 12, 1997.

Bishop, Morris. *Champlain: The Life of Fortitude*. McClelland and Stewart, 1963.

Blackie, Bruce. "Hi-tech Firms in Top 200." The *Ottawa Sun*, May 15, 1997.

—."U of O Gets Hand on SITE." The *Ottawa Sun*, March 20, 1997.

Bond, Courtney C.J. *Where Rivers Meet: An Illustrated History of Ottawa*. Windsor Publications, 1984.

Brown, Karen. "KidsPage." The *Ottawa Citizen*, January 18, 1997.

Chianello, Joanne. "We're Wired." The *Ottawa Citizen*, December 28, 1996.

The Columbia Dictionary of Quotations. New York: Columbia University Press, 1993, 1995.

Durkan, Sean. "Sky's the Limit for Ottawa Airport." The Ottawa Sun, February 17, 1997.

Fletcher, Katherine. "Sunday Best: History through the Eyes of Authors." The *Ottawa Citizen*, May 4, 1997.

Gibbons, Rick. "A Company with Heart." The *Ottawa Sun*, March 10, 1997.

The Great Ottawa Getaway. Toronto: Tait Collins, 1996.

"The Hi-Tech Capital." The *Ottawa Sun*, September 1996.

"High Technology: Ottawa Citizen Semi-Annual Report on High-Tech Companies." The *Ottawa Citizen*, October 1996 and March 1997.

Kirkey, Sharon. "Bryden Backs Artificial Heart Plan." The *Ottawa Citizen*, September 27, 1996.

Laucius, Joanne. "Carp Airport Charts New Course." The *Ottawa Citizen*, November 20, 1996.

Lawson, Catherine. "Program Provides Academic Workout: Colonel By to Offer International Baccalaureate." The *Ottawa Citizen*, March 10, 1997.

McCarthy, Stuart. "Local Job Bonanza." The *Ottawa Sun*, June 7, 1997.

"Meeting Planners Guide." *The Ottawa Business Journal*, February 1997.

Mika, Nick and Helma Mika. *Bytown: The Early Days of Ottawa*. Belleville, Ontario: Mika Publishing Company, 1982.

"Minister Anderson Extends Customs Service at Ottawa Airport." *Revenue Canada*, June 9, 1995.

Moving to Metro Ottawa/Hull. Toronto: Moving Publications Ltd., 1996.

Nortel. "Nortel to Hire 5,000 Knowledge Workers." News Release, June 6, 1997.

Ottawa-Carleton Economic Development Corporation. *Discover the Ottawa You Never Knew!* Ottawa: 1996.

Ottawa-Carleton Economic Development Corporation. *Metro Ottawa Economic Profile 1996*. Ottawa: 1996.

Ottawa-Carleton Economic Development Corporation. *Ottawa: Economic and Community Profile 1997*. Ottawa: 1997.

Ottawa-Carleton Economic Development Corporation and the Corporate Research Group Ltd. *Economic Profile of Metro Ottawa*. Ottawa: 1996.

Ottawa-Carleton Economic Development Corporation and the Corporate Research Group Ltd. *The Ottawa Region Community Economic Profile*. Ottawa: 1997.

Ottawa-Carleton Economic Development Corporation and Future Ottawa. "1996 Submission: *Globe and Mail* Report on *Business Magazine*, Best Cities Report" and "Submission Document: Best Cities Report, *Fortune* Magazine." Ottawa: 1996.

The Ottawa Life Sciences Council, *Life Sciences Sector: 1996 in Review*. Ottawa: 1996.

Ottawa Tourism and Convention Authority. *The Changing Face of Canada's Capital* and *Ottawa at a Glance: Media Information*. Ottawa: 1996.

Ottawa Tourism and Convention Authority. *Ottawa and Canada's Capital Region: Visitors Guide 1996-1997* and *Ottawa and Canada's Capital Region: Destination Planners' Guide 1996*. Ottawa: 1996.

Palladium Corporation (Corel Centre), *Grand Opening* Magazine. Ottawa: 1996.

Taylor, John H. *The History of Canadian Cities*. Canadian Museum of Civilization, Crown Copyright Reserved, 1986.

—.*Ottawa: An Illustrated History*. Canadian Museum of Civilization, Crown Copyright Reserved, 1986.

"Vital Stats: Living in the City." *Newsweek*, January 30, 1995.

WHERE Ottawa-Hull. Toronto: *WHERE* Magazines International, September 1996 and October 1996.

The Works of Samuel de Champlain, Volume II. Toronto: The Champlain Society. Reprint, Toronto and Buffalo: University of Toronto Press, 1971.

Acknowledgments

World Wide Web Resources:

Akran Systems www.akran.ca
Algonquin College www.algonquinc.on.ca
CAL Corporation www.calcorp.com
Calian Technology Ltd. www.calian.com
Canadian Space Agency www.space.gc.ca
Carleton University www.carleton.ca
Caravelle Inc. www.caravelle.com
Cognos Inc. www.cognos.com
Corel Corporation www.corel.com
Council for the Arts in Ottawa
        www.worldlink.ca/~cao
Delta Hotels www.deltahotels.com
Digital Equipment of Canada www.digital.ca
DY 4 Systems www.dy4.com
Fulcrum Technologies www.fulcrum.com
Gandalf Technologies Inc. www.gandalf.ca
Genzyme Corporation www.genzyme.com
Hi-Tech Entrepreneurs Association www.hite.org
i-STAT Corporation www.i-stat.com
JetForm Corporation www.jetform.com
Lockheed Martin www.lmco.com
MITEL Corporation www.mitel.com
Mosaid Technologies Incorporated
        www.mosaid.com
JDS Fitel Inc. www.jdsfitel.com
Lumonics www.lumonics.com
Magma Communications (Virtual Ottawa)
        www.ottawa.com

MDS Nordion www.nordion.com
National Capital Freenet freenet.carleton.ca
National Research Council of Canada
        www.corpserv.nrc.ca
Newbridge Networks www.newbridge.com
Nortel www.nortel.com
Ottawa Business Journal
        www.ottawabusinessjournal.com
Ottawa-Carleton Board of Trade
        www.board-of-trade.org
Ottawa-Carleton Economic Development Corporation
        www.rmoc.on.ca/ocedco
Ottawa-Carleton Learning Foundation
        www.oclf.on.ca
Ottawa-Carleton Research Institute www.ocri.ca
Ottawa Online Ventures ottawa.microworks.ca
Ottawa Tourism and Convention Authority
        www.tourottawa.org
Plaintree Systems www.plaintree.com
QNX Software Systems Ltd. www.qnx.com
Regional Municipality of Ottawa-Carleton
        www.rmoc.on.ca
SHL Systemhouse www.shl.com
Simware www.simware.com
Software Kinetics www.sofkin.ca
Spar Aerospace www.spar.ca
Telesat Canada www.telesat.ca
TMI Communications www.msat.tmi.ca
University of Ottawa www.uottawa.ca

*Additional information provided by
the following organizations:*

Algonquin College
Anglican Diocese of Ottawa
Bank of Canada
Barrymore's Music Hall/Zaphod Beeblebrox
    (Eugene Haslam)
Canadian Museum of Civilization
Canadian Museum of Nature
Carleton University
Casino de Hull
Catholic Immigration Centre–Ottawa
Centrepointe Theatre
Chateau Laurier Hotel
Corel Centre/Palladium Catering Services
Great Canadian Theatre Company

Jewish Community Centre of Ottawa
Jewish Community Council
National Arts Centre
National Capital Commission
National Gallery of Canada
Ottawa-Carleton Board of Trade
Ottawa-Carleton Economic Development Corporation
Ottawa-Carleton Research Institute
Ottawa Congress Centre
Ottawa Life Sciences Council
Ottawa Little Theatre
Ottawa Senators Hockey Club
Ottawa Symphony Orchestra
Ottawa Tourism and Convention Authority
Regional Municipality of Ottawa-Carleton
Roman Catholic Archdiocese of Ottawa
University of Ottawa

The author is grateful to the following:

Columbia University Press for permission to quote Matthew Arnold in *The Columbia Dictionary of Quotations,*
1993, Reprint, New York: Columbia University Press, 1995.

The Champlain Society for permission to quote from *The Works of Samuel de Champlain,*
Volume II. Reprint, Toronto and Buffalo: University of Toronto Press, 1971.

The photographer would like to express deep thanks to the following people:

**Kelly Hamshaw, Dave Caplan, Jim Cochrane, the staff at Ginn Photo, the Camera Exchange II
and my father, Michel, for everything.**

Enterprises Index

Index

This book was set in Helvetica Medium, Bold and Black, Baskerville Regular, Medium, Italic and Medium Italic, Zapf Dingbats and Snell Roundhand Script at Community Communications, Montgomery, Alabama, and printed on 80 lb. Somerset Gloss Text.